Hands-On Cryptography with Python

Leverage the power of Python to encrypt and decrypt data

Samuel Bowne

BIRMINGHAM - MUMBAI

Hands-On Cryptography with Python

Commissioning Editor: Gebin George
Acquisition Editor: Prachi Bisht
Content Development Editor: Deepti Thore
Technical Editor: Varsha Shivhare
Copy Editor: Safis Editing
Project Coordinator: Kinjal Bari
Proofreader: Safis Editing
Indexer: Rekha Nair
Graphics: Jisha Chirayil
Production Coordinator: Nilesh Mohite

First published: June 2018

Production reference: 1280618

Published by Packt Publishing Ltd.
Livery Place
35 Livery Street
Birmingham
B3 2PB, UK.

ISBN 978-1-78953-444-3

www.packtpub.com

`mapt.io`

Mapt is an online digital library that gives you full access to over 5,000 books and videos, as well as industry leading tools to help you plan your personal development and advance your career. For more information, please visit our website.

Why subscribe?

- Spend less time learning and more time coding with practical eBooks and Videos from over 4,000 industry professionals

- Improve your learning with Skill Plans built especially for you

- Get a free eBook or video every month

- Mapt is fully searchable

- Copy and paste, print, and bookmark content

PacktPub.com

Did you know that Packt offers eBook versions of every book published, with PDF and ePub files available? You can upgrade to the eBook version at `www.PacktPub.com` and as a print book customer, you are entitled to a discount on the eBook copy. Get in touch with us at `service@packtpub.com` for more details.

At `www.PacktPub.com`, you can also read a collection of free technical articles, sign up for a range of free newsletters, and receive exclusive discounts and offers on Packt books and eBooks.

Contributor

About the author

Sam Bowne has been teaching computer networking and security classes at City College of San Francisco since 2000. He has given talks and hands-on training at DEFCON, HOPE, B-Sides SF, B-Sides LV, BayThreat, LayerOne, Toorcon, and many other schools and conferences. He has done his PhD and CISSP. He is a DEF CON Black-Badge co-winner.

Packt is searching for authors like you

If you're interested in becoming an author for Packt, please visit authors.packtpub.com and apply today. We have worked with thousands of developers and tech professionals, just like you, to help them share their insight with the global tech community. You can make a general application, apply for a specific hot topic that we are recruiting an author for, or submit your own idea.

Table of Contents

Preface

Cryptography has a long and important history in protecting critical systems and sensitive information. This book will show you how to encrypt, evaluate, compare, and attack data using Python. Overall, the book will help you deal with the common errors in encryption and show you how to exploit them.

Who this book is for

This book is intended for security professionals who want to learn how to encrypt data, evaluate and compare encryption methods, and how to attack them.

What this book covers

Chapter 1, *Obfuscation*, covers the Caesar cipher and ROT13, simple character substitution ciphers, and base64 encoding. We then move on to XOR. In the end, there are challenges to test your learning that involve cracking the Caesar cipher, reversing base64 encoding, and deciphering XOR encryption without the key.

Chapter 2, *Hashing*, covers the older MD5 and the newer SHA hashing techniques and also Windows password hashes. The weakest type of hashing is common use, followed by Linux password hashes, which are the strongest type of hashing in common use. Afterward, there are some challenges to complete. The first is to crack some Windows hashes and recover passwords, then you will be tasked with cracking hashes where you don't even know how many rounds of hashing algorithm were used, and finally you will be asked to crack those strong Linux hashes.

Chapter 3, *Strong Encryption*, covers the primary mode used to hide data today. It is strong enough for the US military. Then, there are two of its modes, ECB and CBC; CBC being the stronger and more common one. We will also discuss the padding oracle attack, which makes it possible to overcome some parts of AES CBC if the designer makes an error and the overly informative error message gives information to the attacker. Finally, we introduce RSA, the main public key algorithm used today, which makes it possible to send secrets over an insecure channel without having exchanged a gives private key. Following all that, we will perform a challenge where, we will crack RSA in the case where it is erroneously created with two similar prime numbers instead of two random prime numbers.

To get the most out of this book

You do not need to have programming experience or any special computer. Any computer that can run Python can do these projects, and you don't need much math because we'll not be inventing new encryption techniques just to learn how to use the pre-existing standard ones that don't require anything more than very basic algebra.

Download the example code files

You can download the example code files for this book from your account at www.packtpub.com. If you purchased this book elsewhere, you can visit www.packtpub.com/support and register to have the files emailed directly to you.

You can download the code files by following these steps:

1. Log in or register at www.packtpub.com.
2. Select the **SUPPORT** tab.
3. Click on **Code Downloads & Errata**.
4. Enter the name of the book in the **Search** box and follow the onscreen instructions.

Once the file is downloaded, please make sure that you unzip or extract the folder using the latest version of:

- WinRAR/7-Zip for Windows
- Zipeg/iZip/UnRarX for Mac
- 7-Zip/PeaZip for Linux

The code bundle for the book is also hosted on GitHub at `https://github.com/PacktPublishing/Hands-On-Cryptography-with-Python`. In case there's an update to the code, it will be updated on the existing GitHub repository.

We also have other code bundles from our rich catalog of books and videos available at `https://github.com/PacktPublishing/`. Check them out!

Download the color images

We also provide a PDF file that has color images of the screenshots/diagrams used in this book. You can download it here: `https://www.packtpub.com/sites/default/files/downloads/HandsOnCryptographywithPython_ColorImages.pdf`.

Conventions used

There are a number of text conventions used throughout this book.

`CodeInText`: Indicates code words in text, database table names, folder names, filenames, file extensions, pathnames, dummy URLs, user input, and Twitter handles. Here is an example: "If we enter `HELLO`, it prints out the correct answer of `KHOOR`."

A block of code is set as follows:

```
alpha = "ABCDEFGHIJKLMNOPQRSTUVWXYZ"
str_in = raw_input("Enter message, like HELLO: ")

n = len(str_in)
str_out = ""

for i in range(n):
    c = str_in[i]
    loc = alpha.find(c)
    print i, c, loc,
    newloc = loc + 3
    str_out += alpha[newloc]
    print newloc, str_out

print "Obfuscated version:", str_out
```

Any command-line input or output is written as follows:

```
$ python
```

Bold: Indicates a new term, an important word, or words that you see onscreen. For example, words in menus or dialog boxes appear in the text like this. Here is an example: "Select **System info** from the **Administration** panel."

Warnings or important notes appear like this.

Tips and tricks appear like this.

Get in touch

Feedback from our readers is always welcome.

General feedback: Email feedback@packtpub.com and mention the book title in the subject of your message. If you have questions about any aspect of this book, please email us at questions@packtpub.com.

Errata: Although we have taken every care to ensure the accuracy of our content, mistakes do happen. If you have found a mistake in this book, we would be grateful if you would report this to us. Please visit www.packtpub.com/submit-errata, selecting your book, clicking on the Errata Submission Form link, and entering the details.

Piracy: If you come across any illegal copies of our works in any form on the Internet, we would be grateful if you would provide us with the location address or website name. Please contact us at copyright@packtpub.com with a link to the material.

If you are interested in becoming an author: If there is a topic that you have expertise in and you are interested in either writing or contributing to a book, please visit authors.packtpub.com.

Reviews

Please leave a review. Once you have read and used this book, why not leave a review on the site that you purchased it from? Potential readers can then see and use your unbiased opinion to make purchase decisions, we at Packt can understand what you think about our products, and our authors can see your feedback on their book. Thank you!

For more information about Packt, please visit packtpub.com.

Obfuscation 1

Python is the best language to start with if you are a beginner, which is what makes it so popular. You can write powerful code with just a few lines, and most importantly, you can handle arbitrarily large integers with complete precision. This book covers essential cryptography concepts; classic encryption methods, such as the Caesar cipher and XOR; the concepts of confusion and diffusion, which determine how strong a crypto system is; hiding data with obfuscation; hashing data for integrity and passwords; and strong encryption methods and attacks against these methods, including the padding oracle attack. You do not need to have programming experience to learn any of this. You don't need any special computer; any computer that can run Python can do these projects. We'll not be inventing new encryption techniques just for learning how to use standard pre-existing ones that don't require anything more than very basic algebra.

We will first deal with obfuscation, the basic idea of what encryption is, and old-fashioned encryption techniques that hide data to make it more difficult to read. This latter process is one of the basic activities that encryption modules use in combination with other methods to make stronger, more modern encryption techniques.

In this chapter, we will cover the following topics:

- About cryptography
- Installing and setting up Python
- Caesar cipher and ROT13
- base64 encoding
- XOR

About cryptography

The term crypto has become overloaded recently with the introduction of all currencies, such as Bitcoin, Ethereum, and Litecoin. When we refer to crypto as a form of protection, we are referring to the concept of cryptography applied to communication links, storage devices, software, and messages used in a system. Cryptography has a long and important history in protecting critical systems and sensitive information.

During World War II, the Germans used Enigma machines to encrypt communications, and the Allies went to great lengths to crack the encryption. Enigma machines used a series of rotors that transformed plaintext to ciphertext, and by understanding the position of the rotors, the Allies were able to decrypt the ciphertext into plaintext. This was a momentous achievement but took significant manpower and resources. Today it is still possible to crack certain encryption techniques; however, it is often more feasible to attack other aspects of cryptographic systems, such as the protocols, the integration points, or even the libraries used to implement cryptography.

Cryptography has a rich history; however, nowadays, you will come across new concepts, such as blockchain, that can be used as a tool to help secure the IoT. Blockchain is based on a set of well-known cryptographic primitives. Other new directions in cryptography include quantum-resistant algorithms, which hold up against a theorized onslaught of quantum computers and quantum key distributions. They use protocols such as BB84 and BB92 to leverage the concepts of quantum entanglement and create good-quality keys for using classical encryption algorithms.

Installing and setting up Python

Python has never been easy to install. In order to proceed, let's make sure that we have set up Python on our machine. We will see how to use Python on macOS or Linux and how to install it on Windows.

Using Python on Mac or Linux

On a macOS or Linux system, you do not need to install Python because it is already included. You just need to open a Terminal window and enter the python command. This will put you in an interactive mode where you can execute python commands one by one. You can close the interactive mode by executing the exit() command. So, basically, to create a script, we use the nano text editor followed by the name of the file. We then enter python commands and save the file. You can then run the script with python followed by the script name. So, let's see how to use Python on macOS or Linux in the following steps:

1. Open the Terminal on a macOS or Linux system and run the python command. This opens an interactive mode of Python, as shown in the following screenshot:

```
test@PPMUMCPU0372:~$ python
Python 2.7.12 (default, Nov 20 2017, 18:23:56)
[GCC 5.4.0 20160609] on linux2
Type "help", "copyright", "credits" or "license" for more information.
>>>
```

2. When you use the print command, it prints Hello right away:

```
>>> print "Hello"
Hello
```

3. We will then leave with the following command:

```
>>> exit()
```

4. As mentioned before, to use Python in interactive mode, we will enter the command as shown:

```
$ nano hello.py
```

5. In the hello.py file, we can write commands like this:

```
print "HELLO"
```

6. Save the file by pressing *Ctrl + X* followed by *Y* and *Enter* only if you've modified it.

7. Now, let's type Python followed by the the script name:

```
$ python hello.py
```

When you run it, you will get the following output:

```
test@PPMUMCPU0372:~$ python hello.py
HELLO
```

The preceding command runs the script and prints out HELLO; that's all you have to do if you have a macOS or Linux system.

Installing Python on Windows

If you have Windows, you have to download and install Python.

Here are the steps which you need to follow:

1. Download Python from https://www.python.org/downloads/
2. Run it in a Command Prompt window
3. Start interactive mode with Python
4. Close with exit()

To create a script, you just use Notepad, enter the text, save the file with *Ctrl + S*, and then run it with python followed by the script name. Let's get started with the installation.

Open the Python page using link given previously and download Python. It offers you various versions of Python. In this book, we will use Python 2.7.12.

Sometimes, you can't install it right away because Windows marks it as untrusted:

1. You have to unblock it in the properties first so that it will run, and run the installer
2. If you go through the steps of the installer, you'll see an optional step named **Add python.exe to path**. You need to choose that selection

The purpose of that selection is to make it so Python can run from the command line in a Terminal window, which is called Command Prompt on Windows.

Now let's proceed with our installation:

1. Open the Terminal and type the following command:

   $ python

2. When you run it, you can see that it works. So, now we will type a command:

   print "HELLO"

   Refer to the following screenshot:

```
test@PPMUMCPU0372:~$ python
Python 2.7.12 (default, Dec  4 2017, 14:50:18)
[GCC 5.4.0 20160609] on linux2
Type "help", "copyright", "credits" or "license" for more information.
>>> print "HELLO"
HELLO
>>>
```

3. We can exit using the `exit()` command as shown earlier.
4. Now, if we want to make a script, we type the following command:

   notepad hello.py

5. This opens up Notepad:

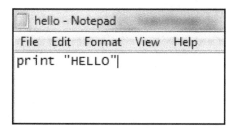

6. We want to create a file. In that file, we enter the following command:

```
print "HELLO"
```

7. Then, save and close it. In order to run it, we need to enter the following command:

```
$ python hello.py
```

It runs and prints HELLO.

Usually, when you install Python on Windows, it fails to correct the path, so you have to execute the following commands to create a symbolic link; otherwise, Python will not start correctly from the command line:

1. `cd c: \Windows`
2. `mklink /H python.exe`
3. `c: \python27\python.exe`

In the next section, we will look at the Caesar cipher and ROT13 obfuscation techniques.

Caesar cipher and ROT13

In this section, we will explain what a Caesar cipher is and how to implement it in Python. Then, we will consider other `shift` values, modular arithmetic, and ROT13.

A Caesar cipher is an ancient trick where you just move every letter forward three characters in the alphabet. Here is an example:

- Plaintext: ABCDEFGHIJKLMNOPQRSTUVWXYZ
- Ciphertext: DEFGHIJKLMNOPQRSTUVWXYZABC

So, HELLO becomes KHOOR.

To implement it, we're going to use the `string.find()` method. The interactive mode of Python is good for testing new methods, hence it's easy to create a string. You can make a very simple script to implement the Caesar cipher with a string named `alpha` for alphabet. You can then take input from the user, which is the plaintext method, then set a value, `n`, which equals the length of the string, and the string out is equal to an empty string. We then have a loop that goes through `n` repetitions, finding the character from string in and then finding the location of that character in the `alpha` string. It then prints out those three values so that we can make sure that the script is working correctly, then it adds 3 to `loc` (location) and puts the corresponding character in string out, and again prints out partial values so that we can see that the script is working correctly. At the end, we print our final output. Adding extra print statements is a very good way to begin your programming because you can detect mistakes.

Implementing the Caesar cipher in Python

Let's go ahead and open the Terminal and follow these steps to implement Caesar cipher in Python:

1. We will use Python in interactive mode first and then make a string that just has some letters in order to test this method:

```
>>> str = "ABCDE"
>>> str.find("A")
0
>>> str.find("B")
1
>>> exit()
```

2. Because we understand how the string methods work, we'll exit and go into the `nano` text editor to look at the first version of our script:

```
$ nano caesar1.py
```

3. When you run the command, you will get the following code:

```
alpha = "ABCDEFGHIJKLMNOPQRSTUVWXYZ"
str_in = raw_input("Enter message, like HELLO: ")

n = len(str_in)
str_out = ""

for i in range(n):
    c = str_in[i]
```

```
    loc = alpha.find(c)
    print i, c, loc,
    newloc = loc + 3
    str_out += alpha[newloc]
    print newloc, str_out

print "Obfuscated version:", str_out
```

You can see the alphabet and the input from the user in the script. You calculate the length of the string, and for each character, `c` is going to be the one character on processing, `loc` will be the numerical location of that character, `newloc` will be `loc` plus 3, and we can then add that character to string out. Let's see this.

4. Leave using *Ctrl+X* and then enter the following command:

   $ python caesar1.py

5. When you run this command, you will get the following output:

   Enter message, like HELLO:

6. If we enter HELLO, it prints out the correct answer of KHOOR:

```
test@PPMUMCPU0372:~$ python caesar1.py
Enter message, like HELLO: HELLO
0 H 7 10 K
1 E 4 7 KH
2 L 11 14 KHO
3 L 11 14 KHOO
4 O 14 17 KHOOR
obfuscated version: KHOOR
```

When we run this script, it takes the input of HELLO and it breaks it up character by character so that it processes each character on a separate line. H is found to be the 7th character, so adding 3 gives me 10, which results in K. It shows us character by character how it works. So, the first version of the script is a success.

To clean the code further, we will remove the unnecessary `print` statements and switch to a `shift` variable. We will create a variable `shift` variable. Which also comes from raw inputs, but we have to convert it to an integer because raw input is interpreted as `text` as you can't add `text` to an integer. This is the only change in the script that follows. If you give it a `shift` value of 3, you get KHOOR; if you give it a `shift` value of 10, you get ROVVY; but if you put in a `shift` value of 14, it crashes, saying string index out of range. Here, the problem is, we've added multiple times to the `loc` variable, and eventually, we move past Z, and the variable is no longer valid. In order to improve that, after adding something to the variable, we'll check to see whether it's greater than or equal to 26, and whether 26 can be subtracted from it. Once you run this, you can use a shift of 14, which will work. We can use a shift of 24, and it works too. However, if we use a shift of 44, it's out of range again. This is because just subtracting 26 once when it's over 26 is not really enough, and the right solution here is modular arithmetic. If we put % 26, it will calculate the number modulus 26, which will prevent it from ever leaving the range of 0 through 25. It will divide it by 26 and keep only the remainder, as expected in this case. We're going to see the modular function many more times as we move forward in cryptography. You can put in any `shift` value of your choice, such as 300, and it will never crash, but will turn that into a number between 0 and 25.

Let's see how the script works with other shift values:

1. Take a look at the script Caesar:

   ```
   $ nano caesar2.py
   ```

2. When you run it, you will get the following:

```
  GNU nano 2.5.3                                    File: caesar2.py
alpha =  "ABCDEFGHIJKLMNOPQRSTUVWXYZ"


str_in = raw_input("Enter message, like HELLO: ")
shift = int(raw_input("Shift value, like 3: "))


n = len(str_in)
str_out = ""


for i in range(n):
    c = str_in[i]
    loc = alpha.find(c)
    newloc = loc + shift
    str_out += alpha[newloc]


print "Obfuscated version:", str_out
```

3. This is the script that allows us to vary the `shift` value but does not handle anything about the `shift` value getting too large. Let's run the following command:

```
$ python caesar2.py
```

4. If you enter HELLO and give it a shift of 3, it's fine, but if we run it again and give it a shift of 20, it crashes:

```
Enter message, like HELLO: HELLO
Shift value, like 3: 20
Traceback (most recent call last):
  File "caesar2.py", line 25, in <module>
    str_out += alpha[newloc]
IndexError: string index out of range
test@PPMUMCPU0372:~$
```

So, as expected, there are some limitations in this one.

5. Let's move on to caesar3:

```
$ nano caesar3.py
```

6. After running it, we get the following output:

```
  GNU nano 2.5.3                              File: caesar3.py

alpha =   "ABCDEFGHIJKLMNOPQRSTUVWXYZ"


str_in = raw_input("Enter message, like HELLO: ")

shift = int(raw_input("Shift value, like 3: "))


n = len(str_in)

str_out = ""


for i in range(n):

  c = str_in[i]

  loc = alpha.find(c)

  newloc = loc + shift

  if newloc >= 26:

    newloc -= 26

  str_out += alpha[newloc]


print "Obfuscated version:", str_out
```

Caesar3 attempts to solve that problem by catching it if we know that the addition causes it to be greater than or equal to 26 and subtracting 26 from it.

7. Let's run the following command:

    ```
    $ python caesar3.py
    ```

8. We will give it shift characters and a shift of 20, and it will be fine:

    ```
    Enter message, like HELLO: HELLO
    Shift value, like 3: 20
    Obfuscated version: BYFFI
    ```

9. If we give it a shift of 40, it does not work:

    ```
    Enter message, like HELLO: HELLO
    Shift value, like 3: 40
    Traceback (most recent call last):
      File "caesar3.py", line 29, in <module>
        str_out += alpha[newloc]
    IndexError: string index out of range
    ```

    There is some improvement, but we are still not able to handle any value of shift.

10. Let's go up to caesar4:

    ```
    $ nano caesar4.py
    ```

11. When you run the command, you will get this:

```
GNU nano 2.5.3                                File: caesar4.py
alpha =  "ABCDEFGHIJKLMNOPQRSTUVWXYZ"


str_in = raw_input("Enter message, like HELLO: ")

shift = int(raw_input("Shift value, like 3: "))


n = len(str_in)

str_out = ""


for i in range(n):

    c = str_in[i]

    loc = alpha.find(c)

    newloc = (loc + shift)%26

    str_out += alpha[newloc]


print "Obfuscated version:", str_out
```

This is the one that uses modular arithmetic with the percent sign, and that's not going to fail.

12. Let's run the following command:

    ```
    $ python caesar4.py
    ```

13. When you run the command, you will get this:

```
Enter message, like HELLO: HELLO
Shift value, like 3: 40
Obfuscated version: VSZZC
test@PPMUMCPU0372:~$ python caesar4.py
Enter message, like HELLO: HELLO
Shift value, like 3: 3000
Obfuscated version: ROVVY
test@PPMUMCPU0372:~$
```

This is the script that handles all the values of the Caesar shift.

ROT13

ROT13 is nothing more than a Caesar cipher with a `shift` equal to 13 characters. In the script that follows, we will hardcode the shift to be 13. If you run one cycle of ROT13, it changes HELLO to URYYB, and if you encrypt it again with the same process, putting in that URYYB, it'll turn back into HELLO, because the first shift is just by 13 characters and shifting by another 13 characters takes the total shift to 26, which wraps right around, and that is what makes this one useful and important:

1. Now let's look at the ROT13 script using the following command:

   ```
   $ nano rot13.py
   ```

2. When you run the preceding command, you can see the script file:

```
  GNU nano 2.5.3                                     File: rot13.py

alpha = "ABCDEFGHIJKLMNOPQRSTUVWXYZ"


str_in = raw_input("Enter message, like HELLO: ")

shift = 13


n = len(str_in)

str_out = ""


for i in range(n):

    c = str_in[i]

    loc = alpha.find(c)

    newloc = (loc + shift)%26

    str_out += alpha[newloc]


print "Obfuscated version:", str_out
```

3. It's just exactly equal to our last Caesar cipher shift, with a script with a shift of 13. Run the script as shown here:

```
$ python rot13.py
```

The following is the output:

```
Enter message, like HELLO: HELLO
Obfuscated version: URYYB
```

4. If we enter the message URYYB and run that, it turns back into HELLO:

```
test@PPMUMCPU0372:~$ python rot13.py
Enter message, like HELLO: URYYB
Obfuscated version: HELLO
```

This is important because there are quite a few cryptographic functions that have this property; where you encrypt something once and encrypt it again, you reverse the process. Instead of making it more encrypted, it becomes unencrypted. In the next section, we will cover base64 encoding.

base64 encoding

We will now discuss encoding ASCII data as bytes and base64 encoding these bytes. We will also cover base64 encoding for binary data and decoding to get back to the original input.

ASCII data

In ASCII, each character turns into one byte:

- A is 65 in base 10, and in binary, it is 0b01000001. Here, you have 0 in the most significant bit because there's no 128, then you have 1 in the next bit for 64 and 1 in the end, so you have *64 + 1=65*.
- The next is B with base 66 and C with base 67. The binary for B is 0b01000010, and for C, it is 0b01000011.

The three-letter string ABC can be interpreted as a 24-bit string that looks like this:

0b01000011	01000010	01000001

We've added these blue lines just to show where the bytes are broken out. To interpret that as base64, you need to break it into groups of 6 bits. 6 bits have a total of 64 combinations, so you need 64 characters to encode it.

The characters used are as follows:

- A, B, C, ... Z   for 0 - 25
- a, b, c, ... z   for 26 - 51
- 0, 1, 2, ... 9   for 52 - 61
- +, /   for 62 and 63

We use the capital letters for the first 26, lowercase letters for another 26, the digits for another 10, which gets you up to 62 characters. In the most common form of base64, you use + and / for the last two characters:

- 'ABC' is   0b01000001 01000010 01000011
- 6-bit groups   0b010000 010100 001001 000011
- Decimal   16   20   9   3
- BASE64   Q   U   J   D

If you have an ASCII string of three characters, it turns into 24 bits interpreted as 3 groups of 8. If you just break them up into 4 groups of 6, you have 4 numbers between 0 and 63, and in this case, they turn into Q, U, J, and D. In Python, you just have a string followed by the command:

```
>>> "ABC".encode("base64")
'QUJD\n'
```

This will do the encoding. Then add an extra carriage return at the end, which neither matters nor affects the decoding.

What if you have something other than a group of 3 bytes?

 The = sign is used to indicate padding if the input string length is not a multiple of 3 bytes.

If you have four bytes for the input, then the base64 encoding ends with two equals signs, just to indicate that it had to add two characters of padding. If you have five bytes, you have one equals sign, and if you have six bytes, then there's no equals signs, indicating that the input fit neatly into base64 with no need for padding. The padding is null.

You take ABCD and encode it and then you take ABCD with explicit byte of zero. x00 means a single character with eight bits of zero, and you get the same result with just an extra A and one equals, and if you fill it out all the way with two bytes of zero, you get capital A all the way. Remember: a capital A is the very first character in base64. It stands for six bits of zero.

Let's take a look at base64 encoding in Python:

1. We will start python up and make a string. If you just make a string with quotes and press *Enter*, it will print it in immediate mode:

    ```
    >>> "ABC"
    'ABC'
    ```

2. Python will print the result of each calculation automatically. If we encode that with base64, we will get this:

    ```
    >>> "ABC".encode(""base64")
    'QUJD\n'
    ```

3. It turns into QUJD with an extra courage return at the end and if we make it longer:

    ```
    >>> "ABCD".encode("base64")
    'QUJDRA==\n'
    ```

4. This has two equals signs because we started with four bytes, and it had to add two more to make it a multiple of three:

```
>>> "ABCDE".encode("base64")
'QUJDREU=\n'
>>> "ABCDEF".encode("base64")
'QUJDREVG\n'
```

5. With a five-byte input, we have one equals sign; and with six bytes of input, we have no more equal signs, instead, we have a total of eight characters with base64.

6. Let's go back to ABCD with the two equals signs:

```
>>>"ABCD".encode("base64")
'QUJDRA==\n'
```

7. You can see how the padding was done by putting it in explicitly here:

```
>>> "ABCD\x00\x00".encode("base64")
'QUJDRAA=\n'
```

There's a first byte of zero, and now we get another single equals sign.

8. Let's put in a second byte of zero:

```
>>> "ABCD\x00\x00".encode("base64")
'QUJDRAAA\n'
```

We have no padding here, and we see that the last characters are all A, indicating that there's been a filling of binary zeros.

Binary data

The next issue is handling binary data. Executable files are binary and not ASCII. Also, images, movies, and many other files have binary data. ASCII data always starts with a zero as the first bit, but base64 works fine with binary data. Here is a common executable file, a forensic utility; it starts with MZê and has unprintable ASCII characters:

```
 AccessData Registry Viewer_1.8.3.exe
   0 4D5A9000 03000000 04000000 FFFF0000  MZê              ˅ ˅
  16 B8000000 00000000 40000000 00000000  ∏          @
  32 00000000 00000000 00000000 00000000
  48 00000000 00000000 00000000 00010000
  64 0E1FBA0E 00B409CD 21B8014C CD215468   ∫   ¥ Õ!∏ LÕ!Th
  80 69732070 726F6772 616D2063 616E6E6F  is program canno
  96 74206265 2072756E 20696E20 444F5320  t be run in DOS
 112 6D6F6465 2E0D0D0A 24000000 00000000  mode.    $
```

As this is a hex viewer, you see the raw data in hexadecimal, and on the right, it attempts to print it as ASCII. Windows programs have this string at the start, and this program cannot be run in DOS mode, but they have a lot of unprintable characters, such as FF and 0, which really doesn't matter for Python at all. An easy way to encode data like that is to read it directly from the file. You can use the `with` command. It will just open a file with filename and mode read binary with the handle `f` and then you can read it. The `with` command is here just to tell Python to open the file, and that if it cannot be opened due to some error, then just to close the handle and then decode it exactly the same way. To decode data you've encoded in this fashion, you just take the output string and you put `.decode` instead of `.encode`.

Now let's take a look at how to handle binary data:

1. We will first exit Python so that we can see the filesystem, and then we'll look for the `Ac` file using the command shown here:

   ```
   >>> exit()
   $ ls Ac*
   AccessData Registry Viewer_1.8.3.exe
   ```

   There's the filename. Since that's kind of a long block, we are just going to copy and paste it.

2. Now we start Python and `clear` the screen using the following command:

   ```
   $ clear
   ```

3. We will start `python` again:

   ```
   $ python
   ```

4. Alright, so, now we use the following command:

```
>>> with open("AccessData Registry Viewer_1.8.3.exe", "rb") as
f:
... data = f.read()
... print data.encode("base64")
```

Here we enter the filename first and then the mode, which is read binary. We will give it filename handle of `f`. We will take all the data and put it in a single variable data. We could just encode the data in `base64`, and it would automatically print it. If you have an intended block in Python, you have to press *Enter* twice so it knows the block is done, and then `base64` encodes it.

5. You get a long block of `base64` that is not very readable, but this is a handy way to handle data like that; say, if you want to email it or put it in some other text format. So, to do the decoding, let's encode something simpler so that we can easily see the result:

```
>>> "ABC".encode("base64")
'QUJD\n'
```

6. If we want to play with it, put that in a `c` variable using the following command:

```
>>> c = "ABC".encode("base64")
>>> print c
QUJD
```

7. Now we can print `c` to make sure that we have got what we expected. We have `QUJD`, which is what we expected. So, now we can decode it using the following command:

```
>>> c.decode("base64")
'ABC'
```

`base64` is not encrypting. It is not hiding anything, but it is just another way to represent it. In the next section, we'll cover XOR.

XOR

This section explains what XOR is on single bits with a truth table, and then shows how to do it on bytes. XOR undoes itself, so decryption is the same operation as encryption. You can use single bytes or multiple byte keys for XOR, and we will use looping to test keys. Here's the XOR truth table:

- 0 ^ 0 = 0
- 0 ^ 1 = 1
- 1 ^ 0 = 1
- 1 ^ 1 = 0

If you feed in two bits and the two bits are the same, the answer is 0. If the bits are different, the answer is 1.

 XOR operates on one bit at a time. Python indicates XOR with the ^ operator.

The truth table shows how it works. You feed in bits that are equally likely to be 0 and 1 and XOR them together, then you end up with 50% ones and zeros, which means that XOR does not destroy any information.

Here's the XOR for bytes:

- A 0b01000001
- B 0b01000010
- XOR 0b00000011

A is the number 65, so you have 1 for 64 and 1 for 1; B is 1 larger, and if you XOR the two of them together, all the bits match for the first 6 bits, and they're all 0. The last two bits are different, and they turn into 1. This is the binary value 3, which is not a printable character, but you can express it as an integer.

The key can be single byte or multibyte. If the key is a single byte, such as B, then you use the same byte to encrypt every plaintext character. Just keep repeating the key over and over:

Single-byte and Multi-byte XOR
• Single-Byte XOR: Use the same key for every byte
• 'ABC' 0b01000001 01000010 01000011
• 'B' repeated 0b01000010 01000010 01000010
• XOR 0b00000011 00000000 00000001

Repeat B for this byte, B for that byte, and so on. If the key is multibyte, then you repeat the pattern:

Multi-Byte XOR: Repeat a pattern
• 'ABC' 0b01000001 01000010 01000011
• 'BC' repeated 0b01000010 01000011 01000010
• XOR 0b00000011 00000001 00000001

You use B for the first byte, C for the next byte, then again B for the next byte, C for the next byte, and so on.

To do this in Python, you need to loop through the bytes of a string and calculate an index to show which byte you're on. Then we enter some text from the user, calculate its length, then go through the indices from 1 up to the length of the string, starting at 0. Then we take the text byte and just print it out here so you can see how the loop works. So, if we give it a five-character plaintext, such as HELLO, it just prints out the characters one by one.

To do the XOR, we'll input a plaintext and a key and then take a byte of text and a byte of key, XOR them together, and print out the results

Note `%len( key)`, which is what prevents you from running off the end of the key. It will just keep repeating the bytes in the key. So, if the key is three bytes long, this will be modulus three, so it will count as 0, 1, 2, and then back to 0 1 2 0 1 2, and so on. In this way, you can handle any length of plaintext.

If you combine uppercase and lowercase letters, you'll often find the case that XOR produces unprintable bytes. In the example that follows, we have used HELLO, Kitty, and a key of qrs. Note that some of these bytes are readily printable and some of them contain strange characters, such as *Esc* and *Tab*, which are difficult to print. Therefore, the best way to handle the output is not to attempt to print it as ASCII, but instead print it as hex encoded values. Instead of trying to print the bytes one by one, we combine them into a `cipher` variable, and in the end, we print out the entire plaintext, the entire key, and then the entire ciphertext in hex. In this way, it can correctly handle these strange values that are difficult to print.

Let's try this looping in Python:

1. We open the Terminal and enter the following command:

    ```
    $ nano xor1.py
    ```

2. When you run it, you will get the following output:

```
  GNU nano 2.5.3                                      File: xor1.py

text = raw_input("Enter text: ")
n = len(text)

for i in range(n):
    t = text[i]
    print t
```

3. This is the first one that is `xor1.py`, so we input text from the user, calculate it's length, and then just print out the bytes one by one to see how the loop works. Let's run it and give it `HELLO`:

```
test@PPMUMCPU0372:~$ python xor1.py
Enter text: HELLO
H
E
L
L
O
```

4. It just prints out the bytes one by one. Now, let's look at the next XOR 2:

```
  GNU nano 2.5.3                                    File: xor2.py

text = raw_input("Enter text: ")
key = raw_input("Enter key: ")
n = len(text)


for i in range(n):
    t = text[i]
    k = key[i%len(key)]
    x = ord(k) ^ ord(t)
    print t, k, x, chr(x)
```

This inputs `text` and `key` the same way and goes through each byte of `text`, picks out the correct byte of `key` using the modular arithmetic, performs the XOR, and prints out the results.

5. So if we run the same file here, we take `HELLO` and a `key` as shown:

```
$ nano xor2.py
$ python xor2.py
```

So, the output is as follows:

```
Enter text: HELLO
Enter key: qrs
H q 57 9
E r 55 7
L s 63 ?
L q 61 =
O r 61 =
```

It calculates the bytes one by one. Note how we get two equals signs here, which is the reason why you would use a multiple by `key` because the plaintext is changing but the key, is also changing and that pattern is not reflected in the output, so it's more effective obfuscation.

6. Clear that and look at the third `xor2a.py` file:

```
GNU nano 2.5.3                                      File: xor2a.py

text = raw_input("Enter text: ")
key = raw_input("Enter key: ")
n = len(text)


cipher = ""
for i in range(n):
    t = text[i]
    k = key[i%len(key)]
    x = ord(k) ^ ord(t)
    cipher += chr(x)
print text, key, cipher.encode("hex")
```

You can see that this handles the problem of unprintable bytes.

7. So, we create a variable named `cipher`, combine each byte of output here, and at the end, we encode it with `hex` instead of trying to `print` it out directly:

```
test@PPMUMCPU0372:~$ python xor2a.py
Enter text: HELLO Kitty
Enter key: qrs
HELLO Kitty qrs 39373f3d3d533a1b07050b
```

8. If you give it `HELLO` and then text a key of `qrs`, it will give you the plaintext `HELLO Kitty`, the key, and then the hexadecimal-encoded output, which can easily handle funny characters, such as 0 7 and 0 5. In the next section, you'll see challenge 1—the Caesar cipher.

Challenge 1 – the Caesar cipher

After a Caesar cipher review, we'll have an example of how to solve it and then your challenge. Remember how the Caesar cipher works. You have an alphabet of available characters, you take in the message and a `shift` value, and then you just shift the characters forward that many steps in the alphabet, wrapping around if you go around the end. The script we end up with works for any `shift` value, including normal numbers, such as 3, or even numbers that are larger than 26; they just wrap around and can scramble any data you put it.

Here's an example:

1. For ciphertext, you can decipher it by just trying all the `shift` values from 0 to 25, and one of them will just be readable. This is a simple brute-force attack. Let's take a look at it.

    Here, in Python, go to the `caesar4` script, that we had before. It takes in a string and shifts it by any value you specify. If we use that script, we can run it as follows:

    ```
    test@PPMUMCPU0372:~$ python caesar4.py
    Enter message, like HELLO: HELLO
    Shift value, like 3: 3
    Obfuscated version: KHOOR
    ```

2. Then, if we put in HELLO and shift it by 3, it turns into KHOOR.

3. If we want to crack it, we can use the solution script as follows:

```
GNU nano 2.5.3                              File: caesar5.py

alpha =  "ABCDEFGHIJKLMNOPQRSTUVWXYZ"
str_in = raw_input("Enter ciphertext: ")

for shift in range(26):


  n = len(str_in)
  str_out = ""


  for i in range(n):
    c = str_in[i]
    loc = alpha.find(c)
    newloc = (loc + shift)%26
    str_out += alpha[newloc]


  print shift, str_out
```

4. So, if we use that script, we can run it:

```
test@PPMUMCPU0372:~$ python caesar5.py
Enter ciphertext: KHOOR
0  KHOOR
1  LIPPS
2  MJQQT
3  NKRRU
4  OLSSV
5  PMTTW
6  QNUUX
7  ROVVY
8  SPWWZ
9  TQXXA
10 URYYB
11 VSZZC
12 WTAAD
13 XUBBE
14 YVCCF
15 ZWDDG
16 AXEEH
17 BYFFI
18 CZGGJ
19 DAHHK
20 EBIIL
21 FCJJM
22 GDKKN
23 HELLO
24 IFMMP
25 JGNNQ
test@PPMUMCPU0372:~$
```

5. If we put it in KHOOR, it'll shift it by a variety of values, and you can see the one that's readable at 23, which is HELLO. So, the example we discussed before of longer ciphertexts and so on will become readable down at 3, where you see its DEMONSTRATION:

```
Enter ciphertext: ABJLKPQOXQFLK
0  ABJLKPQOXQFLK
1  BCKMLQRPYRGML
2  CDLNMRSQZSHNM
3  DEMONSTRATION
4  EFNPOTUSBUJPO
5  FGOQPUVTCVKQP
6  GHPRQVWUDWLRQ
7  HIQSRWXVEXMSR
8  IJRTSXYWFYNTS
9  JKSUTYZXGZOUT
10 KLTVUZAYHAPVU
11 LMUWVABZIBQWV
12 MNVXWBCAJCRXW
13 NOWYXCDBKDSYX
14 OPXZYDECLETZY
15 PQYAZEFDMFUAZ
16 QRZBAFGENGVBA
17 RSACBGHFOHWCB
18 STBDCHIGPIXDC
19 TUCEDIJHQJYED
20 UVDFEJKIRKZFE
21 VWEGFKLJSLAGF
22 WXFHGLMKTMBHG
23 XYGIHMNLUNCIH
24 YZHJINOMVODJI
25 ZAIKJOPNWPEKJ
```

6. Your challenge is to decipher this string: MYXQBKDEVKDSYXC.

In the next section, we'll have a challenge on base64.

Challenge 2 – base64

After a base64 review, we'll perform an example to show you how to decode some obfuscated text, and then we have one simple and one hard challenge for you.

Here is the `base64` review:

> - Encode with **.encode("base64")**
> - Decode with **.decode("base64")**

`base64` encoding text makes it longer. Here's the sample text to decode:

U2FtcGxiHRleHQ=

It decodes into the string sample text. Let's take a look at that.

Refer to the following steps:

1. If you run `python` in immediate mode, it will do four simple jobs:

   ```
   $ python
   ```

2. So, if we take ABC and encode it with `base64`, we get this string:

   ```
   >>> "ABC".encode("base64")
   'QUJD\n'
   ```

3. If we decode that with `base64`, we get back to the original text:

   ```
   >>> "QUJD".decode("base64")
   'ABC'
   ```

4. So, the challenge text is as follows, and if you decode it, you get the string sample text:

   ```
   >>> "U2FtcGxiHRleHQ=".decode("base64")
   'Sample text'
   ```

5. So, that will do for simple case; your first challenge looks like that:

   Decode this: VGhpcyBpcyB0b28gZWFzeQ==

6. Here's a long string to decode for your longer challenge:

   Decode this:
   VWtkc2EwbEliSFprVTJeF16S1ZaMWxxUUW5OaU1qbDNVSGM5UFFvPQo=

This long string is so long because it's been encoded by `base64` not just once but several times. So, you'll have to try decoding it until it turns into something readable. In the next section, we'll have *Challenge 3 – XOR*.

Challenge 3 – XOR

In this section, we will review how XOR works and then give you an example, and then present you with two challenges.

So, here is one of the XOR programs we discussed before:

```
  GNU nano 2.5.3                                        File: xor2.py

text = raw_input("Enter text: ")
key = raw_input("Enter key: ")
n = len(text)


for i in range(n):
    t = text[i]
    k = key[i%len(key)]
    x = ord(k) ^ ord(t)
    print t, k, x, chr(x)
```

You input arbitrary texts and an arbitrary key, and then go through the bytes one by one, picking out one byte of text and one byte of key before combining them with XOR and printing out the results. So, if you put in `HELLO` and `qrs`, you'll get encrypted stuff, encrypted with XOR.

Here's an example:

> - Ciphertext: **snw{fzs**
>
> - Key is **6**

It will scramble into `EXAMPLE`. So, this undoes encryption; remember that XOR undoes itself.

If you want to break into one of these, one simple procedure is just to try every key and print out the results for each one, and then read the key is readable.

So, we try all single-digit keys from 0 to 9.

The result is that you feed in the ciphertext, encrypt it with each of these, and when you hit the correct key value, it will turn into readable text.

Let's take a look at that:

```
  GNU nano 2.5.3                                        File: xor3.py

text = raw_input("Enter text: ")
n = len(text)


for k in "0123456789":
    clear = ""
    for i in range(n):
        t = text[i]
        x = ord(k) ^ ord(t)
        clear += chr(x)
    print k, clear
```

Here's the decryption routine, which simply inputs texts from the user and then tries every key in this string, 0 through 9. For each one of those it combines, think the XORed text into a variable named `clear`, so it can print one line for each key and then the clear result. So, if we run that one and put in my ciphertext, it gives us 10 lines.:

```
test@PPMUMCPU0372:~$ nano xor3.py
test@PPMUMCPU0372:~$ python xor3.py
Enter text: snw{fzs
0 C^GKVJC
1 B_FJWKB
2 A\EITHA
3 @]DHUI@
4 GZCORNG
5 F[BNSOF
6 EXAMPLE
7 DY@LQMD
8 KVOC^BK
9 JWNB_CJ
```

We just scanned through these lines and saw which one becomes readable, and you can see the correct key and the correct plaintext at 6. The first challenge is here:

> • Decipher this: **kquht}**
>
> • Key is a single digit

This is similar to the one we saw earlier. The key is a single digit, and it will decrypt into something readable. Here's a longer example that is in a hexadecimal format:

> • Decipher this: **70155d5c45415d5011585446424c**
>
> • Key is two digits of ASCII

The key is two digits of ASCII, so you'll have to try 100 choices to find a way to turn this into a readable string.

Summary

In this chapter, after setting up Python, we covered the simple substitution cipher, the Caesar cipher, and then base64 encoding. We gathered data six bits at a time instead of eight bits at a time, and then we looked at XOR encoding, where bits are flipped one by one in accordance with the key. We also saw a very simple truth table. The challenges you performed were cracking the Caesar cipher without the key, cracking base64 by reversing it to get the original bytes, and cracking XOR encryption without knowledge of the key with a brute-force attack trying all possible keys. In Chapter 2, *Hashing*, we will cover different types of hashing algorithms.

2
Hashing

Hashing has two main purposes: the first is to put a fingerprint on a file so you can tell whether it has been altered, and the second is to conceal passwords so you can still recognize the correct password and enable login but a person who steals the hash cannot easily recover the password from it.

In this chapter, we will cover the following topics:

- MD5 and SHA hashes
- Windows password hashes
- Linux password hashes
- Challenge 1 – cracking Windows hashes
- Challenge 2 – cracking many-round hashes
- Challenge 3 – cracking Linux hashes

MD5 and SHA hashes

After explaining what a hash function is, we will deal with MD5 and then the SHA family: SHA-1, SHA-2, and SHA-3. We will also acquire a bit of information about cracking hashes.

What are hashes?

As mentioned earlier, one point of using hashes is to put a fingerprint on a file. You can take all the bytes in the file and combine them together with a hash algorithm, and this creates a fixed-links hash value. If you change any part of the file and recalculate the hash, you get a completely different value. So, the idea is that if you have two files that are supposed to be identical, you can calculate the hash of each file, and if the hash of both files match, then the files are identical.

A very common hash is MD5; it's been around for a couple of decades. It's 128 bits long, which is rather short for a hash function, and it's reliable enough for most purposes. People use it to put a fingerprint on downloads, and malware samples, and all sorts of things, and they are also sometimes used to obscure passwords. It's not a perfect hash function: there are some collisions known, and there are some algorithms that, at the expense of some computer time, can create collisions, which are pairs of files that hash to the same value. So, if you do find two files with MD5s that match, you do not know with complete certainty that they are identical files, but they usually are.

It's very easy to calculate them in Python. You just import the hash library and then proceed with the calculation. You call the hash library to create a new object. The first parameter is the algorithm used, which is MD5. The second parameter is the contents of the data to be hashed.

Here, we will use HELLO as an example, and then you need to use the hex-digest at the end or it will just print an address to the data structure instead of showing you the actual value. We will use the hash of HELLO, MD5, and a hexadecimal and it is 128 bits long. So, that's 128 over 4, or 32, hexadecimal characters, and if you add another character to the HELLO, like an exclamation point the hash changes completely; there's no resemblance between the hash of one value and the hash of the next.

The **Secure Hash Algorithm (SHA)** was designed to be an improvement on MD5, and SHA-1 had no collisions until about a year ago, when some researchers at Google Inc. found out how to make collisions in SHA-1, so careful people are switching to SHA-2. There is another algorithm approved by the **National Institute of Standards**, called **SHA-3**, which almost nobody is using because as far as anyone expects, SHA-2 will remain secure for a very long time to coms. But, if something were to happen to compromise SHA-2, SHA-3 will be available for us to use. Both SHA-2 and SHA-3 have various lengths, but the most common lengths are 256 and 512 bits.

You can calculate SHA-1 and SHA-2 hashes easily in Python, but SHA-3 is not commonly used and it's not part of this hash library yet. So, if you use SHA-1 for the algorithm, you get a SHA-1 hash. It looks like an MD5 hash, but it's longer. Then there are SHA-256 and SHA-512, which are both SHA-2 hashes. You can see that, although they're more secure, they are much longer and somewhat less convenient:

```
>>> import hashlib
>>> hashlib.new("sha1", "HELLO").hexdigest()
'c65f99f8c5376adadddc46d5cbcf5762f9e55eb7'
>>> hashlib.new("sha256", "HELLO").hexdigest()
'3733cd977ff8eb18b987357e22ced99f46097f31ecb239e878ae63760e83e4d5'
>>> hashlib.new("sha512", "HELLO").hexdigest()
'33df2dcc31d35e7bc2568bebf5d73a1e43a0e624b651ba5ef3157bbfb728446674a231b8b6e97fa1e570c3b1de6d6c677541b262ac22afda5878fa2b591c7f08'
>>>
```

So, let's take a look.

Open the Terminal and execute the `python` command to start the Python Terminal:

```
test@PPMUMCPU0372:~$ python
Python 2.7.12 (default, Nov 20 2017, 18:23:56)
[GCC 5.4.0 20160609] on linux2
Type "help", "copyright", "credits" or "license" for more information.
>>>
```

You can then run the following commands:

```
>>> import hashlib
>>> hashlib.new("md5", "HELLO").hexdigest()
'eb61eead90e3b899c6bcbe27ac581660'
>>> hashlib.new("md5", "HELLO!").hexdigest()
'9ac96c64417b5976a58839eceaa77956'
>>>
```

You have to import `hashlib`. Then, you can add `hashlib.new`. The first parameter is the algorithm, which is `md5`, in this case. The next parameter is the data to hash, which is `HELLO`, and then `hexdigest` is added to see the hexadecimal value. So, there's the hash of `HELLO`, and if we put another character at the end such that it reads `HELLOa`, then we get a completely different answer:

```
>>> hashlib.new("md5", "HELLOa").hexdigest()
'f017243288f24f851a43c07328318733'
>>>
```

If we want to use a different algorithm, we can just put in SHA-1:

```
>>> hashlib.new("sha1", "HELLO").hexdigest()
'c65f99f8c5376adadddc46d5cbcf5762f9e55eb7'
>>>
```

Now we get a long hash, and, if we add `sha256` as character, we get an even longer hash:

```
>>> hashlib.new("sha256", "HELLO").hexdigest()
'3733cd977ff8eb18b987357e22ced99f46097f31ecb239e878ae63760e83e4d5'
>>>
```

These are enough hashes for almost any purpose.

If you have the hash value of something and you want to calculate the data it came from, in principle, there is not a unique solution. In practice, though, for short objects like passwords, there is. So, if someone uses an MD5 function to obscure a password, which is done by some old web applications, then you can reverse it by guessing passwords until you find a match. There is no mathematical way to undo a hash function, so you just have to make a library. In the example of the MD5 hash of HELLO, if you just made a series of guesses, you'd get the right answer. That's how hash cracking works; it's not a complicated idea, it's just kind of inconvenient.

We can take the MD5 hash of HELLO and keep guessing:

```
test@PPMUMCPU0372:~$ python
Python 2.7.12 (default, Nov 20 2017, 18:23:56)
[GCC 5.4.0 20160609] on linux2
Type "help", "copyright", "credits" or "license" for more information.
>>> import hashlib
>>> hashlib.new("md5", "HELLM").hexdigest()
'078975f7ae348a9b44872ef330f52cd5'
>>> hashlib.new("md5", "HELLN").hexdigest()
'42a761cb17ea0ad153a2244553f1ed02'
>>> hashlib.new("md5", "HELLO").hexdigest()
'eb61eead90e3b899c6bcbe27ac581660'
>>>
```

If we were guessing words, we might have to guess millions of words to get down to the value shown, but if we are able to guess the right value, we'll know it's right when the hash matches. The only thing that determines the difficulty of this is how many hashes you can calculate per second, and MD5 and the SHA family are designed to calculate very fast, so you could actually try millions of passwords per second with them. In the next section, we'll talk about Windows password hashes.

Windows password hashes

In this section, we will see how to get hashes with Cain and then how MD4 and Unicode work. Then, we'll discuss cracking hashes with Google and cracking hashes with wordlists.

Getting hashes with Cain

Cain is a free hacking tool that can harvest Windows hashes from a running operating system. In order to test it, we'll make three accounts on Windows Server, the very latest version of the Windows operating system. You can use the user command at the Command Prompt to do this. You can add a user named `John` with a password `P@sw0rd`, a user named `Paul` with a password, and a user named `Ringo` with password `P@sw0rd999`:

```
Administrator: Command Prompt

C:\Users\Administrator>net user /? able P@sw0rd
The syntax of this command is:

NET USER
[username [password | *] [options]] [/DOMAIN]
          username {password | *} /ADD [options] [/DOMAIN]
          username [/DELETE] [/DOMAIN]
          username [/TIMES:{times | ALL}]
          username [/ACTIVE: {YES | NO}]


C:\Users\Administrator>net user john P@sw0rd /add
The command completed successfully.


C:\Users\Administrator>net user paul P@sw0rd /add
The command completed successfully.


C:\Users\Administrator>net user ringo P@sw0rd999 /add
The command completed successfully.
```

If you run Cain, it can harvest the hashes. The following screenshot shows the three users and their hashes:

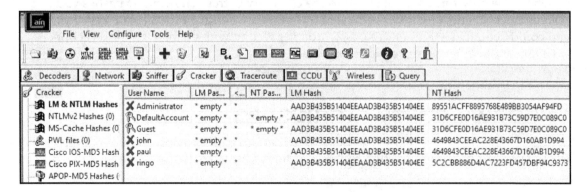

The **LM Hash** section is an obsolete system that is no longer used by any version of Windows, so it just contains a dummy value that has no information. The actual hash used by Windows when you log in is called the **NT Hash**. Notice that if two users have the same password, they have exactly the same hash: a 464 value. That is one of the weaknesses in this system. It is a very weak and old password system, unfortunately.

MD4 and Unicode

Here's the algorithm Microsoft uses. It takes the password and encodes in Unicode instead of ASCII, and then when you run it through MD4 (which is a very old algorithm, even older than MD5), it produces the NT hash value:

```
>>> hashlib.new("md4", "P@sw0rd".encode("utf-16le")).hexdigest()
'4649843ceeac228e43667d160ab1d994'
>>> 
```

The reason Unicode is used is because Microsoft is an international operating system that allows you to have passwords in languages such as Chinese and Japanese that do not encode with 8-bits per character but 16-bits per character.

Cracking hashes with Google

Since password hashes have no variation and any two users with the same password will have the same hash, all the hackers that had cracked wordlists for the last 24 years have put their results on the internet, resulting in a situation where you can just Google frequently used password hashes:

If you just put a hash into Google, you'll often find that somebody has already cracked it for you and put on the internet. For instance, here's this one P@sw0rd that's got a known result, so you can crack it. That simple method works for a great many passwords but this technique does not work for the password, we used for the user Ringo, which is P@sw0rd999.

Cracking hashes with wordlists

So, in a case where the passwords cannot be cracked, you need to calculate it yourself:

```
>>> for c in "6789":
...     p = "P@sw0rd99" + c
...     h = hashlib.new("md4", p.encode("utf-16le")).hexdigest()
...     print p, h
...
P@sw0rd996 b3ef8f811b362bf13045afd2f5716baf
P@sw0rd997 ffeb5fe830aa227428073fcb1aa15c59
P@sw0rd998 9f630141e0b30b0cc41a4dd1352bd9bd
P@sw0rd999 5c2cbb886d4ac7223fd457dbf94c9373
>>>
```

You just use the same procedure. Make a series of guesses, hash them, and hunt for your answer. If your list of guesses does eventually hit the right value, you'll of course find it here. So, you can see the password P@sw0rd999 with 5c2c....

It's very simple, so let's give it a try in Python.

In the Terminal window, we'll enter the python command. Next we'll import the hashlib library:

```
test@PPMUMCPU0372:~$ python
Python 2.7.12 (default, Nov 20 2017, 18:23:56)
[GCC 5.4.0 20160609] on linux2
Type "help", "copyright", "credits" or "license" for more information.
>>> import hashlib
>>> hashlib.new("md4", "P@sw0rd".encode("utf-16le")).hexdigest()
'4649843ceeac228e43667d160ab1d994'
>>>
```

Thus, you can see the line that does the encoding. We put in the password, encode utf-16le, which is the Unicode; then, we hash it with MD4 and express it as hexdigest.

That's number for `P@sw0rd`. Now, if we try to get to the `Ringo` user, we need to have a list of two hashes to try, which will need to have some values that eventually reach the right value:

```
>>> hashlib.new("md4", "P@s0rd".encode("utf-16le")).hexdigest()
'8af4abf869c655bdec3e0709c0cf9244'
>>> hashlib.new("md4", "P@sw0rd997".encode("utf-16le")).hexdigest()
'ffeb5fe830aa227428073fcb1aa15c59'
>>> hashlib.new("md4", "P@sw0rd998".encode("utf-16le")).hexdigest()
'9f630141e0b30b0cc41a4dd1352bd9bd'
>>> hashlib.new("md4", "P@sw0rd999".encode("utf-16le")).hexdigest()
'5c2cbb886d4ac7223fd457dbf94c9373'
>>>
```

If we are just counting up sequentially using `997`, `998`, and `999`, we'll get that `5c2c...` value that we are looking for.

Linux password hashes

In this section, we will first discuss how to get the hashes from an operating system, and then look at the salting and stretching procedures that make Linux hashes much stronger. We will then discuss the specific hashing algorithm used by modern versions of Linux, and finally look at cracking hashes with wordlists and Python.

Here, we have created three users to test the software in much the same way as we did earlier on Windows. `John` and `Paul` have the same password and `Ringo` has a different password:

```
student@ubuntu:~$ sudo tail -n 3 /etc/shadow
john:$6$qIo0foX5$r7kx5FnTYMWANoz8zacMRdHjxiFs9aaKsj2nObFOzS.q86AfOVCxJKH/kqdcDrT
FH9XvSXQ5ZDEmcEzX2NCik/:17447:0:99999:7:::
paul:$6$yoHEm7/a$XUBKbMwYa3V5QPLGL4tsL3yNiGD7Bx5v1grn.sVQfxFp0aLGNPFW51OQYTvtMtE
MNGC.tpBtwu/GPM4SDhp5W.:17447:0:99999:7:::
ringo:$6$yOb0ojJ/$CIHCzyqDq1hhR1fJ3nR9AOiIqvA0XUycbWH1e4QQ/QCt/beFyzFe98AJVoAr/a
LYz2ShRVYwfYY.cKVnnupcP.:17447:0:99999:7:::
```

You get the hashes from the `/etc/shadow` file, from which we will print out the last three records. So, you will see `John`, `Paul`, and `Ringo`, and after each username comes `$6`, which indicates that it is a type 6 of password, which is the most modern and secure form. Then there is a long, random string of characters that goes up to the next dollar sign, and then an even longer random string of characters, which is the password hash itself.

The first thing you can see is the password hash, which is much longer and more complicated than the Windows password hash. The next thing to observe is that even though John and Paul have the same password, they have completely different hashes, because it adds a random salt to each one before hashing them in order to obscure the fact that these passwords are the same, making the passwords much stronger. Salting is the procedure of adding random characters before hashing; stretching is also employed here. Instead of just using one round of MD4, it uses 5,000 rounds of SHA-512, which simply makes it take much more CPU time to calculate the hash. The point of this is to slow down attackers who are trying to make dictionaries of password hashes.

You can find the details of the method in the /etc/login.defs file, which shows you that modern versions of Linux using crypt methods SHA512 and 5000 rounds:

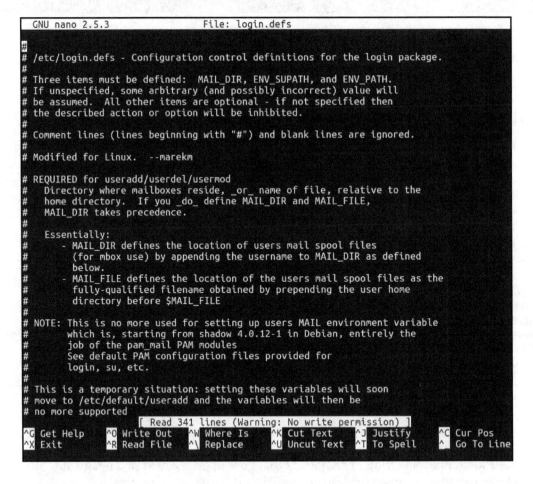

Thus, the procedure requires you to combine `salt` with the password. You perform an algorithm that includes 5,000 rounds of SHA-512 hashing. It actually has more than 20 steps that involve taking two hashes together and mixing the bits together, but it's a little more complicated than just repeating the same hash algorithm over and over.

We'll use the `passlive` library. Before using it in Python, you have to install it with the `pip install passlib` command. Once you've got it, you can import the `sha512_crypt` module. Here's how you use it:

```
>>> import hashlib
>>> from passlib.hash import sha512_crypt
>>> sha512_crypt.using(salt="qIo0foX5", rounds=5000).hash("P@sw0rd")
'$6$qIo0foX5$r7kx5FnTYMWANoz8zacMRdHjxiFs9aaKsj2nObFOzS.q86AfOVCxJKH/kqdcDrTFH9XvSXQ5ZDEmc
zX2NCik/'
>>>
```

Let's start the Python Terminal. Then we can import the `passlib` library as shown earlier, because we've already put it in `pip install`.

Now, we can calculate the first one, which will use the `salt` value from the shadow file and hash it, as shown in the previous screenshot.

As you can see, we get the correct results (starting `r7k`). And, if we were doing a dictionary attack, we would have a series of password guesses as shown:

```
>>> sha512_crypt.using(salt="qIo0foX5", rounds=5000).hash("P@sw0ra")
'$6$qIo0foX5$DX/.gSq2C8NdzBK9Yn2lWTLMw3nQw1pRebYEBaasuyEioRFImk9tF1cHIlC9Ecmdnk6QZFuYnkUXWk
.6Jssbo0'
>>> sha512_crypt.using(salt="qIo0foX5", rounds=5000).hash("P@sw0rb")
'$6$qIo0foX5$iYl6BYzTCgWTdRl5ErYB/EoL4ImlwwPBMqDrLDSVomCvLG83Id8oAAkrFixSzxoKtmu79qBLa6JDK6
irIMwLj0'
>>> sha512_crypt.using(salt="qIo0foX5", rounds=5000).hash("P@sw0rc")
'$6$qIo0foX5$FJnTG1I0aaR2Z7MadTzSG90WaL57vC8Jta./DKLw9f6vhHdi9BXThneeocx0e5hYKTJJIrT17uOzkB
WNwGhdQ/'
>>> sha512_crypt.using(salt="qIo0foX5", rounds=5000).hash("P@sw0rd")
'$6$qIo0foX5$r7kx5FnTYMWANoz8zacMRdHjxiFs9aaKsj2nObFOzS.q86AfOVCxJKH/kqdcDrTFH9XvSXQ5ZDEmcE
zX2NCik/'
>>>
```

It's just a question of trying them until you get the one that matches.

Challenge 1 – cracking Windows hashes

After a review of Windows hashing and an example of 1-digit hashing, we will give you two challenges—one with a 2-digit password and one with a 7-digit password. Here's how Windows hashes look in Python:

```
>>> hashlib.new("md4", "P@sw0rd".encode("utf-16le")).hexdigest()
'4649843ceeac228e43667d160ab1d994'
>>>
```

The algorithm uses `hashlib` to do an MD4 for the hash of the password, but before you do that, encode in Unicode which is `utf-16le`, and then calculate the `hexdigest` of the results to get the long number, The number starts with `464`, in this case, which is a Windows password hash.

Thus, you can write a program that will try all the characters in this string, which will consist of 10 digits, and then calculate the hash for each one of them. You will be left with a simple dictionary with 10 values:

```
GNU nano 2.5.3                     File: chal1a.py

import hashlib

for c1 in "0123456789":
  p = c1
  hash = hashlib.new("md4", p.encode("utf-16le")).hexdigest()
  print p, hash
```

You can crack this 1-digit hash using a 1-digit password as follows:

```
test@PPMUMCPU0372:~$ python chal1a.py
0 7bc26760a19fc23e0996daa99744ca80
1 69943c5e63b4d2c104dbbcc15138b72b
2 8f33e2ebe5960b8738d98a80363786b0
3 5f18a8499cdd4f43d89424ad39ce9af7
4 e30f7b55215aa69b2920e3715e0392a0
5 94f23786fe827d0a3c0029dc5eb27a65
6 c7c0f6f33f4e34bc0b595fc942cb6d03
7 b3cc27d02c5e59ac39384440fdfff0fd
8 99ce74551ba6bfb12eac366090e26032
9 90ad6ab281c4ae016e5a7564c307a7e8
test@PPMUMCPU0372:~$
```

So, here's a challenge. The password is a 2-digit one between 00 and 99, and this is the hash:

> Hash:
>
> ○ 5875F2524BBE45F3504236B75A9A483D

So, you have to make a loop that tries 100 possible values.

The next one is a 7-digit password, and this is the hash:

> Hash:
>
> ○ 0342DB37D0A08A6EA2284584876CCED0

So, you'll have to try 10 million values. That will only take a few seconds, and that's why Windows password hashes are so very weak—you can try many millions of them per second.

Challenge 2 – cracking many-round hashes

After a review of how MD5 and SHA work in Python, we will see what a many round hash is, and then you will get two challenges to solve.

MD5 and SHA are both easy to calculate:

```
test@PPMUMCPU0372:~$ python
Python 2.7.12 (default, Dec  4 2017, 14:50:18)
[GCC 5.4.0 20160609] on linux2
Type "help", "copyright", "credits" or "license" for more information.
>>> import hashlib
>>> hashlib.new("md5", "password").hexdigest()
'5f4dcc3b5aa765d61d8327deb882cf99'
>>> hashlib.new("sha1", "password").hexdigest()
'5baa61e4c9b93f3f0682250b6cf8331b7ee68fd8'
>>>
```

From the `hashlib` library, you just need to use the `hashlib.new` method and put the name of the algorithm in the first parameter, the password in the second parameter, and then add the hex-digest to it to see the actual result in hexadecimal instead of just an address to the object. To do many rounds, you just repeat that process.

You need to put the password in `h` and then use the current `h`, to calculate the next `h` and repeat this over and over and over. Here's a little script that prints out the first 10 rounds of a multi-round MD5 hash:

```
test@PPMUMCPU0372:~$ python
Python 2.7.12 (default, Dec  4 2017, 14:50:18)
[GCC 5.4.0 20160609] on linux2
Type "help", "copyright", "credits" or "license" for more information.
>>> import hashlib
>>> p = "password"
>>> h = p
>>> for i in range(10):
...     h = hashlib.new("md5", h).hexdigest()
...     print i+1, h
...
1 5f4dcc3b5aa765d61d8327deb882cf99
2 696d29e0940a4957748fe3fc9efd22a3
3 5a22e6c339c96c9c0513a46e44c39683
4 e777a29bee9227c8a6a86e0bad61fc40
5 7b3b4de00794a247cf8df8e6fbfe19bf
6 20ffe80a69fbe8ce4d848eef461b3e39
7 55ae17202f23e50f30883ee4bb581001
8 c66bfc320be01d07d4c326dea4254cb9
9 97265ae89ab509a0e969a024b73f8e1e
10 e36b70041d8f1609aa40b9ebba4363cf
>>> █
```

This technique is called **stretching**, and it's used by stronger password hashing routines, such as the Linux password hashes that we've seen in previous sections.

Here's your first challenge: a 3-digit password hashed 100 times with MD5. Find it from this hash:

c09145ad46b058fba82e4218169c7121

Here's another challenge for you. In this one, you have an unknown number of rounds with SHA-1, but it's not more than 5,000. So, you just have to try all values and find the 3-digit password of the results in this hash.

Challenge 3 – cracking Linux hashes

After a review of Linux hashes, we'll show you your challenge.

Linux hashes are salted and stretched, and there are various versions of them. We are covering the current version, which is version 6, that is, the most secure form:

```
>>> from passlib.hash import sha512_crypt
>>> s = "12345678"
>>> p = "password"
>>> sha512_crypt.using(salt=s, rounds=5000).hash(p)
'$6$12345678$I8tr4xFAC6/TtjYWdp0LWEjQre2LcYm2jdSMNLQDIyqRv.cKo7KMD5/HpzVVFKpUQlIekr/Vw.OdIm
tRM85fg/'
>>> 
```

The hash is a long string starting with the dollar sign; the 6 indicates the version, then you have a dollar sign followed by salt, and another dollar sign followed by the hash. To calculate them in Python, you need to import a special SHA-512 crypt library, as you use the format shown earlier.

Here's your third challenge: a 3-digit password in this format. The salt value is penguins and the hash is this long mess starting with a P instance.

Summary

In this chapter, we covered the MD5 and SHA-1 hashing algorithms, the Windows password hashing algorithm, and the Linux password hashing algorithm. In the challenges, you cracked a Windows password hash to recover a plaintext password, and another password hash using an unknown number of MD5 and SHA-1 rounds. Finally, you cracked the Linux password hashes to recover the plaintext password.

In Chapter 3, *Strong Encryption*, we will cover two main methods of strong encryption, that is, AES and RSA.

3
Strong Encryption

Strong encryption conceals data even against determined adversaries, such as enemy military agencies, if done correctly. The two main methods of strong encryption are AES and RSA, which are both approved by the US government. You do not need to have programming experience to learn this, and you don't need any special computer; any computer that can run Python can do these projects. Also, you don't need much math because we are not going to be inventing new encryption techniques just to learn how to use the standard pre-existing ones that don't require anything more than very basic algebra.

In this chapter, we will cover pre-existing:

- Strong encryption with AES
- ECB and CBC modes
- Padding oracle attack
- Strong encryption with RSA
- What's next?

Strong encryption with AES

In this section, we will take a look at the **Advanced Encryption Standard** (**AES**), private key encryption, key and block size, how to influence AES, and Python and confusion and diffusion.

AES is the encryption standard approved by the United States National Institute of Standards and is considered very secure. It's approved even for the storage of secret military information. It is private key cryptography, which is the kind of cryptography that has been used for thousands of years in which both the sender and the receiver use the same key. It's a block cipher, so the input data has to be put in blocks that are 128-bits long, and a block of plaintext is encrypted with a key, producing a block of ciphertext:

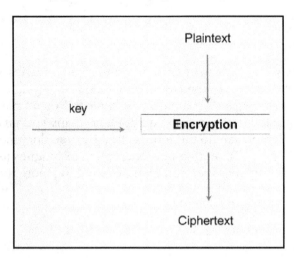

There are three key sizes: 128, 192, and 256-bits. The most common type of AES is the 128-bit key size, and that's what we'll use in this example. In Python, it's quite easy to use.

Firstly, you need to import the AES module from `crypto cipher`, then you need a 16-byte key and plaintext, which is some integral multiple of 16 bytes. You will then create a new AES object with the key and then calculate it with cipher encrypt. This gives you a 16-byte string, which may be unprintable, so it's best to encode it as hex to print it out; and, of course, if you decrypt it, you get back to your original plaintext. This has many desirable cryptographic properties, and one of them is confusion. If you change a bit of the key, it changes the entire ciphertext.

So, if we change the key to `kex`, you will see that all of the ciphertext changes. This is what you want. Two very similar keys produce completely different results, so you cannot find any pattern in the results that you could use to deduce information about the key.

Similarly, diffusion is a desirable property, where if you encrypt something twice with the same key but you change even one bit of the plaintext, again, the entire ciphertext changes. See the following example:

```
>>> key    = "Sixteen byte key"
>>> cipher = AES.new(key)
>>> cipher.encrypt("Secret: 16 bytes").encode("hex")
'433811598181fed6d59e265249f8c6a8'
>>>
>>> cipher.encrypt("Secret: 16 bytet").encode("hex")
'90c106728883ece4a2470a352c0865d2'
```

Here we have bytes and we get the same `433` ending in `6a8`. If we change the last letter to `t`, you can see that it starts with `90c` and ends with `5d2`; that is, it completely changes.

Let's take a look at that in Python:

1. Open the Terminal window and start `python`. We will enter the following command, as shown in the sceenshot:

```
test@PPMUMCPU0372:~$ python
Python 2.7.12 (default, Dec  4 2017, 14:50:18)
[GCC 5.4.0 20160609] on linux2
Type "help", "copyright", "credits" or "license" for more information.
>>> from Crypto.Cipher import AES
>>> key = "Sixteen byte key"
>>> plain = "Secret: 16 bytes"
>>> cipher = AES.new(key)
>>> ciphertext = cipher.encrypt(plain)
>>> print ciphertext.encode("hex")
433811598181fed6d59e265249f8c6a8
>>>
```

2. We import the AES module, where we have a 16-byte key and a 16-byte plaintext. We have created an AES object, encrypted it, and then we have printed out the hex value over here:

```
433811598181fed6d59e265249f8c6a8
>>>
```

3. Now, we change the key:

```
>>> key = "Sixteen byte kez"
>>> cipher = AES.new(key)
>>> ciphertext = cipher.encrypt(plain)
>>> print ciphertext.encode("hex")
b0f907cd312776f66727efb29d197494
>>>
```

Here we go up to the key line and change that to say z, and then do it again, creating a new AES object with that key. Performing the encryption and printing out the results again, you see everything is different.

It now starts with b, ends with 4, and has completely changed.

4. Now, we'll leave the key where it is and change the plaintext. Let's change t to F. Now if we encrypt that and print out the result in hexadecimal, once again, everything has changed; even though this is the same key as the one above it:

```
>>> plain = "Secret: 16 bytfs"
>>> ciphertext = cipher.encrypt(plain)
>>> print ciphertext.encode("hex")
051b203ab814f0975955352268ed3812
>>>
```

So, this shows both confusion and diffusion, which are desirable properties. In the next section, we'll discuss ECB and CBC modes.

ECB and CBC modes

We'll compare **Electronic Codebook (ECB)** and **Cipher Block Chaining (CBC)** and show you how to implement AES CBC in Python.

ECB

In the ECB method, each block of plaintext is encrypted with the key separately, so if you have two blocks of plaintext that are the same, they will result in identical ciphertext:

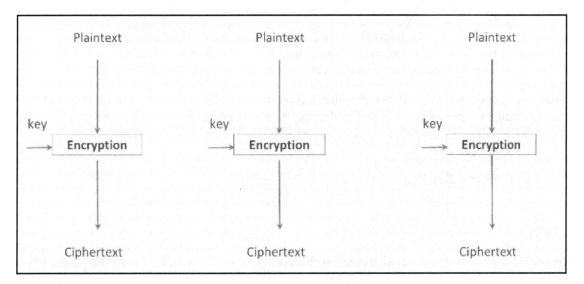

If you have something like an image here with large areas of solid colors such as gray and black and then you encrypt it, you'll just get different colors but the pattern won't change:

That's not good. You can still see that this is a picture of a penguin, and that's not what most people expect out of encryption. You expect the encryption to conceal the data so attackers looking at the encrypted data can't tell what the message is, and here that property is not present.

Thus, CBC is considered the best solution to this problem.

CBC

In addition to the key, you add an initialization vector, which is XOR'd with the plaintext before encryption. Then for the next block, you take the ciphertext produced by encryption and use it as the initialization vector for the second block. The output of that is used as the initialization vector for the third block. Thus, even if the inputting plaintext is the same in every block, the ciphertext will be different in each block:

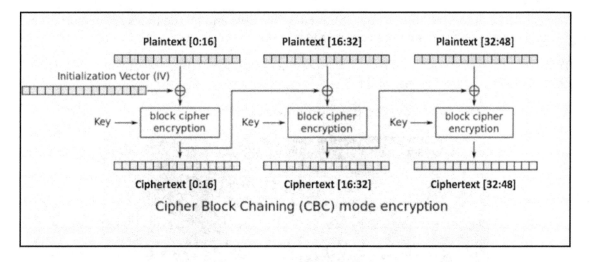

Cipher Block Chaining (CBC) mode encryption

This results in far more obfuscation:

You can see that the penguin is now completely invisible and all the bytes are just random, so this is preferred from almost every purpose.

To do it in Python, here's how we did the previous AES, which was the EBC mode. By default, you don't specify the mode.

If you want to use CBC mode, you put the following command:

```
>>> from Crypto.Cipher import AES
>>> key = "Sixteen byte key"
>>> iv = "Initialization v"
>>> plain = "Secret: 16 bytfs"
>>> cipher = AES.new(key, AES.MODE_CBC, iv)
>>> cipher.encrypt(plain).encode("hex")
'0aae623c4b42bb3b8011dde45e0fdc71'
>>>
```

AES mode CBC when you create the cipher object. You also have to provide an initialization vector, which can be 16 bytes, just like the key. If you encrypt one block of 16 bytes of text, there's no obvious difference in the result because of the initialization vector, but it's just a block of hexadecimal. To see the effect of this, you need to make the plaintext longer. When you encrypt it, you get a blob of hexadecimal. That's the ECB mode, which does not remove all the patterns in the data. Here's the CBC mode with the same repeating input. As you can see, the output has no pattern, and does not repeat however far you go. So, it much more effectively conceals the data.

Let's take a look at that. We start Python in the Terminal, and then add this code:

```
test@PPMUMCPU0372:~$ python
Python 2.7.12 (default, Dec  4 2017, 14:50:18)
[GCC 5.4.0 20160609] on linux2
Type "help", "copyright", "credits" or "license" for more information.
>>> from Crypto.Cipher import AES
>>> key = "Sixteen byte key"
>>> plain = "Secret: 16 bytes"
>>> cipher = AES.new(key)
>>> ciphertext = cipher.encrypt(plain)
>>> print ciphertext.encode("hex")
433811598181fed6d59e265249f8c6a8
```

So, you can see the 16-byte key and the 16-byte plaintext AES in ECB mode. We encrypt it and print the answer.

If we want to make it longer, we add this:

```
>>> plain3 = 3*plain
>>> plain3
'Secret: 16 bytfsSecret: 16 bytfsSecret: 16 bytfs'
>>>
```

You can multiply a string object in Python and if you just print it out, you'll see it's just the same thing three times.

Now we can encrypt that `plain3`:

```
>>> ciphertext = cipher.encrypt(plain3)
>>> print ciphertext.encode("hex")
788afe6ac36a4503a3d3388fdba8e6d1628b31a513bd5252e5f079d714b3ab99b5a84c2d7c04be121fdf9e9fe2ced02b
>>>
```

When we print that out, it'll have that repeating pattern for 33. Now, if we change the mode, we'll need an `iv`:

```
>>> iv = "1111222233334444"
>>> cipher = AES.new(key, AES.MODE_CBC, iv)
>>> ciphertext = cipher.encrypt(plain3)
>>> print ciphertext.encode("hex")
```

We just need 16 bytes, so we'll just 16 bytes to `iv`. Next, we create a new `AES` object. In the `iv` now, we encryp `plain3` again, and we print out the result again.

You see it has `61f`, and you can see that there's no longer any repetition. So, this is a much more effective way to encrypt things if you really want to obscure the input.

Padding oracle attack

In this section, we will see how padding works in the PKCS # 7 system and then show you a system with the `PADDING ERROR` message. Plus, we'll also deal with the padding oracle attack, which makes it possible to craft ciphertext that will decode 20 plaintext we want.

Here is the encryption routine:

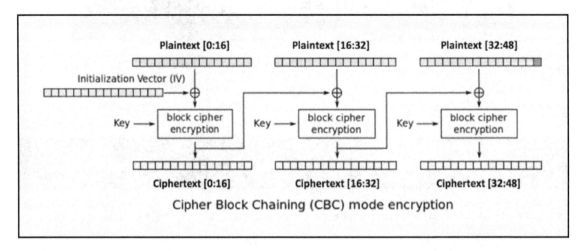

Cipher Block Chaining (CBC) mode encryption

We'll have three blocks of data, each 16-bytes long. We'll encrypt the data with AES in CBC mode, so in comes the initialization vector and the key. You produce three blocks of ciphertext, and each one of the blocks after the first uses the output of the previous encryption routine as an initialization vector to XOR with the plaintext.

Here's how PKCS#7 padding works:

- If one byte of padding is needed, use `01`
- If two bytes of padding are needed, use `0202`
- If three bytes of padding are needed, use `030303`
- And so on...

If we have a message here that is only 47-bytes long, then we can't fill the last block, so we have to add a byte of padding. You could use a variety of numbers as the padding, but in this system, we use one binary value one, if you have one byte of padding needed if you have two, you use two for both bytes and three for all three bytes for three bytes of padding and so on. This means that, if we decrypt it, we'll have three blocks of ciphertext. We decrypt it and we'll get the 47-byte message:

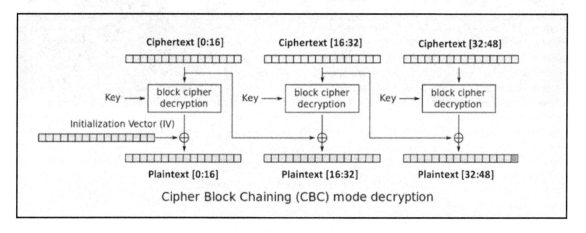

Cipher Block Chaining (CBC) mode decryption

The last byte here will always be the padding byte, and that will be 0-1, a binary value of 1.

Here is an example of a vulnerable system that you can attack. This is just using the same techniques we've made before where we just encrypt things with AES and CBC mode, which you can save in `pador.py`, and then you can just import it to make it easy to use and more realistic. There have been real systems that use this. So, we import, encrypt, and decrypt methods so that we can put in a 47-pipe message and encrypt it. We'll get a long blob of hexadecimal output.

If we decrypt that, we will get our original input plus one byte of 01 at the end. x01 is the Python notation for a single byte with the binary value of 1. If you modify the input by keeping the first 47 bytes alone and changing the last byte to A or 65 and decrypt it, you'll get a padding error. This error message may seem harmless, but in fact it makes it possible to completely subvert the encryption.

Let's take a look at that:

1. Open the Terminal and start `python`.
2. We will enter the following command:

```
test@PPMUMCPU0372:~$ python
Python 2.7.12 (default, Dec  4 2017, 14:50:18)
[GCC 5.4.0 20160609] on linux2
Type "help", "copyright", "credits" or "license" for more information.
>>> from pador import encr, decr
>>> a = "This is simple sentence is forty-seven bytes long."
>>> c = encr(a)
>>> print c.encode("hex")
```

3. We will encrypt and decrypt routines. You can see we have the plaintext. When we encrypt 47 bytes of plaintext, we get a long binary blob:

> 941dc2865db9204c40dd6f0898cbe0086fc6d915e288ed4ef223766a02967b8
> 1c6c431778a40f517e9e4aa86856e0a3b68297e102b1ec93713bf89750cdfa8
> 0e

4. When we decrypt that, we get the following:

```
>>> decr(c)
'This is simple sentence is forty-seven bytes long.\x0e\x0e\x0e\x0e\x0e\x0e\x0e\x0e\x0e\x0e\x0e\x0e\x0e\x0e'
```

We can see that it in fact added the single byte of padding at the end of it.

Now, we should do the deformed one. If we set our modified text equal to the original plaintext going up to character `47` and then we add `"A"` at the end, when we decrypt it, we get `'PADDING ERROR'`:

```
>>> mod = a[:47] + "A"
>>> decr(mod)
'PADDING ERROR'
>>>
```

That is the error message that we can exploit to subvert the system. So, here's how the padding oracle attacked works change:

1. Change ciphertext [16:31] to any bytes
2. Change ciphertext [31] until padding is valid
3. Intermediate [47] must be 1

Here is a diagram of CBC:

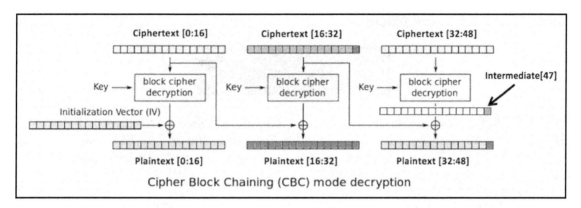

Leave the first 16 bytes of the ciphertext alone. Change this to anything you like, such as all-As, and then decrypt that. What will happen is, because you changed the bytes in the second block, the second block will turn to random characters, and so will the third block. But it'll give you a padding error unless the, very last byte of the very last block is one. So, you brute force it. You change a byte to all 256 possible values until the byte becomes 1, and when that happens, you know this value is 1. You know this value because it's the one that did not give you a padding error message, and you can XOR them to determine this intermediate value right here. So, proceeding byte by byte to the left, you can determine these intermediate values. If you know them, you can put in ciphertext that will make anything you like appear in the third block. So, you can defeat the encryption even though you don't know the key or the initialization vector.

Here's the code that does it:

```
>>> prefix = c[0:16] + "A"*15
>>> for i in range(256):
...     mod = prefix + chr(i) + c[32:]
...     if decr(mod) != "PADDING ERROR":
...         print i, "is correctly padded"
...
```

And will get the following output:

```
255 is correctly padded
>>> 234 ^ 1
235
```

We set the ciphertext equal to the first original 16 bytes of ciphertext and then 15 bytes of A. Then we vary the next byte through all possible 256 values and add the third block of data unchanged. After that, we look to see when we no longer get a padding error, and that will be 234, so the intermediate value is 234 XOR one:

1. Now, if we want to get the next byte back, we have to arrange two bytes of padding, both of which will be 2, as shown:

   - Two bytes of padding:
     - ciphertext[46] =ciphertext[47] = 2
     - Set ciphertext[31] = 235 ^ 2 = 233

   So, the final two bytes of ciphertext 46 and 47 will both be two. So, we set ciphertext 31 to the value needed to create two there. Now that we know the intermediate value, we can calculate it.

2. We vary ciphertext 30 until the padding is valid and that will determine the next byte of the intermediate:

```
>>> prefix = c[0:16] + "A"*14
>>> for i in range(256):
...     mod = prefix + chr(i) + chr(233) + c[32:]
...     if decr(mod) != "PADDING ERROR":
...         print i, "is correctly padded"
...
```

3. Leave the first block unchanged and add 14 bytes of a vary the next byte. Leave the byte at the chosen value of 233 so you know that the final byte of the decrypted output will be 2, and when the padding error message goes away, you can take that number, XOR it with 2, and you get the next value of the intermediate. So, now we can make messages. We would have to repeat this more times to get more bytes, but for this demonstration, we'll settle for a message just one letter long. We'll make an A followed by a binary value of 1 for valid padding. That's our goal, and in order to do that, all we have to do is set ciphertext 30 and 31 to these chosen values:
   - ciphertext[30] = ord("A") ^ 113
   - ciphertext[31] = 16 235

4. Since we know the intermediate values are 113 and 235, we just need to XOR these intermediate values with the values we want.

5. We will create ciphertext that will decrypt to a message ending in A and a binary 1, so let's see that go. Now, this one is a little complicated, so we've chosen to save some of the text here in a text editor so we can do it stage by stage:

```
from pador import encr, decr
a = "This simple sentence is forty-seven bytes long."
c = encr(a)
print c.encode("hex")
decr(c)

mod = c[0:47] + chr(65)
decr(mod)

from pador import encr, decr

prefix = c[0:16] + "A"*15
for i in range(256):
    mod = prefix + chr(i) + c[32:]
    if decr(mod) != "PADDING ERROR":
        print i, "is correctly padded"


prefix = c[0:16] + "A"*14
for i in range(256):
    mod = prefix + chr(i) + chr(233) + c[32:]
    if decr(mod) != "PADDING ERROR":
        print i, "is correctly padded"


prefix = c[0:16] + "A"*14
c30 = ord("A") ^ 113
c31 = 1 ^ 235
mod = prefix + chr(c30) + chr(c31) + c[32:]
decr(mod)
```

6. Here's our Python:

```
>>> from pador import encr, decr

>>> prefix = c[0:16] + "A"*14
>>> for i in range(256):
...     mod = prefix + chr(i) + chr(233) + c[32:]
...     if decr(mod) != "PADDING ERROR":
...         print i, "is correctly padded"
```

7. Alright, we import the library, which we already had anyway. Here we leave the first 16 bytes unchanged and fill in 15 bytes with A. Then, we have the loop that changes the next byte's every possible value and leave the third block of data unchanged. We run through the loop until we no longer get a padding error. This tells us that 234 is the value that gives us correct padding:

234 is correctly padded

8. So, we take 234 to the 1, which tells us the intermediate value, all over cut the indentation right, so it's 234 XOR 1. This tells us that the value is 235. That's the intermediate value. For the next bit, use a very similar process, so now we have 14 bytes of padding. We will vary the next byte, and the byte after that is 233, which is chosen to always give us a 2 at the end. So, when we run this loop through, it is correctly padded at 115:

```
...
```
115 is correctly padded

9. So, 115 XOR 2 is 113:

```
>>> 115 ^ 2
113
```

Therefore, 113 is the next byte of intermediate value.

10. Now that we know these two numbers, 235 and 113, we can control the last two bytes of plaintext. Now we will keep the first block of input data unchanged. We have 14 bytes of padding:

```
>>> prefix = c[0:16] + "A"*14
>>> c30 = ord("A") ^ 113
>>> c31 = 1 ^ 235 mod = prefix + chr(c30) + chr(c31) +
c[32:]
>>> decr(mod)
```

11. We choose to make A and a binary one with the two bytes, 235 and 113. When we create the modified ciphertext and decrypt it, we get the following message:

```
"This simple
sent\xc6\x8d\x12;y.\xdc\xa2\xb4\xa9)7c\x95b\xd1I\xd0(\xbb\x1f\x
8d\xebR1Y'\x17\xf6wA\x01"
```

The first block of data is unmodified. The second block and most of the third block have changed to random characters, but we controlled the last two bytes and we could make them say anything we wanted. So, we are able to create ciphertext that will decrypt at least partly two values we choose, even though we don't know the key or the initialization vector.

Strong encryption with RSA

In this section, we will cover public key encryption, the RSA algorithm, and implementation in Python.

Public key encryption

In public key encryption, we solve this problem: Google, for example, wants to receive confidential data from users, such as passwords and credit card numbers, but they don't have a secure communication channel; what they have is the public internet, and any data being sent might be eavesdropped upon by any number of attackers. Thus, there's no way to deliver a shared secret key, and symmetric encryption algorithms, such as AES, cannot solve this problem. That's where public key encryption comes in.

Google creates a key pair. They keep the private key secret and don't tell anyone, and they publish public key so anyone can know it. Everyone who wants to send secrets to Google can encrypt them with the public key and send them over an insecure channel because the only one who can decrypt them is Google, who has the private key. Mailboxes work like this. Anybody can go to the mailbox and put mail in the top slot, but the bottom door is locked, and only the postal worker with the private key can take the mail out. The private key and the public key must be related, but they have to be related by a one-way function so that it's easy to calculate the public key from the private key, which is what Google has to do when they first set up their key pair. But it has to be very difficult to calculate the private key from the public key, so it's safe to publish the public key and no one's going to find the private key.

RSA algorithm

There are various one-way functions that can be used for this purpose, but in RSA, the function is factoring a large number:

- Private key d is made from two large prime numbers: p and q
- Public key is the product of n = p * q, and and arbitrary value e
    - If p and q are large, factoring n into p and q is very difficult

If you multiply the two prime numbers p and q together to create their product n, it is a well-known difficult problem to factor n into p and q. And if p and q are large enough, it becomes essentially impossible. This is the one-way function. You can easily multiply p and q to create the public key n, but knowledge of the public key cannot be used to determine p and q practically:

- **Public key**: This is two numbers, (n,e)
    - e can be any prime number, often 65537
- **Encryption**: $y = x^e \bmod n$
- **Decryption**: $x = y^d \bmod n$
    - x is plaintext, y is ciphertext

So, the public key is n, which is the product of two prime numbers and another arbitrary number, e, which is often just this value 65,537. Anyone who wishes to secretly send their plaintext, x, raises it to the power of e, modulus n, and sends that scrambled stuff over an insecure channel, such as the internet, to the recipient. The recipient has the private key so they can find the decryption key, d, and they take the ciphertext to d modulus n, and that turns into the decrypted message. The decryption key is calculated this way:

- phin = (p-1) * (q-1)
- d*e = 1 mod phin

Since Google knows the p and q secrets, they can calculate this number phin which is p – 1, times q – 1 and then they choose a decryption key so that d times e is 1 modulus Phi of n. Nobody else can do this calculation because they do not know the values of p and q. So, in Python, you can import the RSA module and then generate a key of whatever length you like. In this example, we have used 2048 bits, which is the current National Institute of Standards recommendation. Then, they have a public key. There's a message to encrypt and you encrypt it, and the result is this very long ciphertext, which is as long as 2048 bits. ciphertext is long and the calculations are very slow, so you do not normally send a long message with this method. What you do in RSA is just send a secret key, and then you use AES to encrypt everything after that point to make the calculations faster. This chapter covers something called textbook RSA, which contains many of the essential ingredients but is not really secure enough for real use, because you have to add a padding that is specified in RFC 8017. This adds a hash value, a mask, and padding to the message and protects the key from some attacks. Let's take a look at this in Python.

Implementation in Python

Here is how we can implement what we've talked about in Python:

1. We start up python and then add the following code:

```
test@PPMUMCPU0372:~$ python
Python 2.7.12 (default, Dec  4 2017, 14:50:18)
[GCC 5.4.0 20160609] on linux2
Type "help", "copyright", "credits" or "license" for more information.
>>> from Crypto.PublicKey import RSA
>>> key = RSA.generate(2048)
>>>
```

2. The last step shown takes around 2 to 4 seconds just to generate the key; that's because it had to find two large prime numbers, and these are very difficult calculations:

```
>>> publicKey = key.publickey()
>>> plain = 'encrypt this message'
>>> ciphertext = publicKey.encrypt(plain, 0)[0]
>>> print ciphertext.encode("hex")
```

3. It has to guess a number and test it, and typically, it has to try more than a hundred guesses for each of these large prime numbers, so this process is very time-consuming. However, it happens automatically, and now we can encrypt the message with the key, producing this very long ciphertext:

```
4ac8816ed69452a9f574deee72173a8881db6cfe5bc8bf6c11513105cccc06e4446fdd6d19146694deb507ca86cffa4c9c3d214578902f062cee337417fc0ec27ac
0ece9ab225deac588a9c9191c3e14147dd3656e1ddecd4dd2001db1da670f5122b77436609cc1fd356e5f33fa91adf22f0fbb82af140189a9ee75b8dcde85c9691e
535f1ea303b3836b0d0eb142662bb3ad064b660952049b276ec2ba83efd6f9eb7b39696c16cd01882f2f4ea9cc62f47c5beab6b090915e3c4fc2ff644913286372e
82fa735b90db0c1d9b39933db7cfff1497498aac2e184e679b665666f61f5317ab8e91dd71db7698c0a19c70be30e2c9a85ad9666ce206cf82f7578
```

4. Now, we could test this to see whether we change one bit of the message or take the plaintext and change that last letter to an f. If we encrypt that, the results will be similar to the following:

```
>>> plain = 'encrypt this messagf'
>>> ciphertext = publicKey.encrypt(plain, 0) [0
... ciphertext = publicKey.encrypt(plain, 0) [0
keyboardInterrupt
>>> ciphertext = publicKey.encrypt(plain, 0) [0]
>>> print ciphertext.encode ("hex")
```

5. Now, we print the results:

```
1dc722865cc796a47de57bf94ff531c1b07127f15f5c0fb1eb4f7e31f0292ac0c381e4c2badf608080fe60018a8779d472d44c7ab34bb5df0e744b5eeafed320dc7
ba840ddbde2cf0c6888debac5e3da3b27e561929a56245739033dfd9e5b49baa6c85e6825556257f7c76632606fe3934ca4d1aa5f98a2db444f972aa2cff718cacf
24ceab784c8b767eba2110e7061a4fdf243302f32aaf26398ad6fccc3ace1d1d42f73c68f0d426fc446984cd646c73751b8fb1391d9568e2c1ad8e5dac9915511bc
74313c4567d855a552bc9dbd1db27b47475ae713520e806314f47f884511173686f5df157186a2a360256e002cf7bafe3ee85cbda68098a371e0f4633
```

As you can see, all 4ac go to 1dc, and then it ends at 578 to 633. This is the desirable property of strong encryption. Any change in the input changes all of the output clipping approximately half the bits.

Challenge – cracking RSA with similar factors

In this section, we will cover topics such as large integers–in Python and the decimal library. We will also take a look at an example of factoring a large number and then two challenges for you to solve.

Large integers in Python

Python can do multiplication and division–and a contented multiplication and division of arbitrarily large integers with complete precision:

```
>>> a = 1001
>>> a*a
1002001
>>> a = 10**100 + 1
>>> a
10000000000000000000000000000000000000000000000000000000000000000000000000000000000000000000000000001L
>>> a*a
100000000000000000000000000000000000000000000000000000000000000000000000000000000000000000000000000020000000000000000000000000000000000000000000000000000000000000000000000000000000000000000000000000000000001L
>>>
```

If we have 1001 and then we calculate 1001 squared, we get the right answer, of course; and even if we take a number like 10**100 + 1, it correctly gets that number a hundred places with a 1 at each end. Now, if we square that number, it again gets it correct, all the way to the one at each end.

So, for simple integer operations, Python's precision is unlimited. However, if we want to square root, we need to import a math library:

```
>>> a = 10**100 + 1
>>> b = a*a
>>> import math
>>> math.sqrt(b)
1e+100
>>>
```

The math library does not keep any arbitrary number of places, as you can see in the preceding code. If we take 10 **100 + 1 and square it, then take the square root, we don't get 10 **100 + 1. We get 10 ** 100, which means it rounded off to some number of places less than 100, and that's fine for many purposes. However, it's not fine for what we want to do here, which is factor large integers.

In order to do that, you use the decimal library, and we will import it as shown:

```
>>> from decimal import *
>>> a = 10**100 + 1
>>> b = a*a
>>> Decimal(b).sqrt()
Decimal('1.000000000000000000000000000E+100')
>>> getcontext().prec = 200
>>> Decimal(b).sqrt()
Decimal('10000000000000000000000000000000000000000000000000000000000000000000000000000000000000000000000000001')
```

As you can see, we have imported the decimal library and set value to a as 10 **100+ 1. Here b equals to a squared, and then instead of calculating the square root of b with the math library, you calculate the decimal value of b with the decimal library. Use the square root method of that and this gives you again the wrong answer, because by default, the decimal library rounds things off. But if you set the precision to be higher, you get exactly the right answer, and that's why the decimal library is better for our purposes. This getcontext().prec command lets us set it to keep enough places to be as precise as we want.

All right, so, you wouldn't be able to factor a large number in the general case, and that's what makes RSA secure. But, if a mistake is made by using numbers and can be predictable in some way, then RSA can be cracked:

Example:

o 10000000000000000001680000000000000000005031

```
>>> n = 10000000000000000001680000000000000000005031
>>> getcontext().prec = 50
>>> Decimal(n).sqrt()
Decimal('100000000000000000083.99999999999999998987500000000')
```

Here the mistake is using two prime factors that are close together instead of choosing independent random numbers for the two prime factors. So, this large number is the product of two prime factors, and so you can factor it. So, if we put that number in a value called n, we set the precision to 50 places and calculate the square root. We find that the square root is 1 followed by many zeros, and that is ended at 83 +a fraction.

Now, if the number is the product of two prime numbers, and the two prime numbers are close together, one number must be less than the square root and the other number must be larger than the square root.

So, if we simply start at the square root and try numbers close to the square root by jumping back by two every time, we will eventually find the prime factor, and we do:

```
>>> for p in range(1000000000000000000083, 1000000000000000000030, -2):
...     print p, n%p
...
1000000000000000000083 9999999999999998059
1000000000000000000081 9999999999999998065
1000000000000000000079 9999999999999998079
1000000000000000000077 9999999999999998101
1000000000000000000075 9999999999999998131
1000000000000000000073 9999999999999998169
1000000000000000000071 9999999999999998215
1000000000000000000069 9999999999999998269
1000000000000000000067 9999999999999998331
1000000000000000000065 9999999999999998401
1000000000000000000063 9999999999999998479
1000000000000000000061 9999999999999998565
1000000000000000000059 9999999999999998659
1000000000000000000057 9999999999999998761
1000000000000000000055 9999999999999998871
1000000000000000000053 9999999999999998989
1000000000000000000051 9999999999999999115
1000000000000000000049 9999999999999999249
1000000000000000000047 9999999999999999391
1000000000000000000045 9999999999999999541
1000000000000000000043 9999999999999999699
1000000000000000000041 9999999999999999865
1000000000000000000039 0
1000000000000000000037 184
1000000000000000000035 376
1000000000000000000033 576
1000000000000000000031 784
```

Of course, we can jump back by twos because even numbers are certainly not prime, so we don't need to test the even numbers.

And, as we can see, now we've found a number where the modulus of n modulus the number is zero, so this is a prime factor.

We can get the other prime factor by just dividing n by the first one:

```
>>> n = 100000000000000000168000000000000000005031
>>> p = 100000000000000000039
>>> q = n/p
>>> q
100000000000000001289L
>>>
>>> p*q
100000000000000000167900000000000000050271L
```

So, here's the original number, n, which is the product of two primes, and we have one of the primes; q is n over p which you can see. To test it, if we calculate p*q, we get the original number again. So, we have factored a large number into p and q, and that is enough information to crack RSA.

So, let's try that in Python. Go to the Terminal and run `python`:

```
>>> n = 100000000000000000168000000000000000005031
>>> from decimal import *
>>> getcontext().prec = 50
>>> Decimal(n).sqrt()
```

So, we have n equal to the large number shown. We import this number to the `decimal` library and set the position to 50 places. Now, if we take the square root, we get 1 followed by many zeros, and then 83, and then a fraction. Then, we copy the integer part of the square root:

```
Decimal('10000000000000000083.99999999999999998987500000000')
```

Now we set p in range of that number followed by the number, as shown here:

```
>>> for p in range(10000000000000000083, 10000000000000000030, -2):
```

This begins a loop, and all we have to do is print:

```
...     print p, n%p
...
```

It will calculate n modulus p, which will be zero. If that's an integral multiple, pressing *Enter* twice runs the loop:

```
. . .
100000000000000000083  99999999999999998059
100000000000000000081  99999999999999998065
100000000000000000079  99999999999999998079
100000000000000000077  99999999999999998101
100000000000000000075  99999999999999998131
100000000000000000073  99999999999999998169
100000000000000000071  99999999999999998215
100000000000000000069  99999999999999998269
100000000000000000067  99999999999999998331
100000000000000000065  99999999999999998401
100000000000000000063  99999999999999998479
100000000000000000061  99999999999999998565
100000000000000000059  99999999999999998659
100000000000000000057  99999999999999998761
100000000000000000055  99999999999999998871
100000000000000000053  99999999999999998989
100000000000000000051  99999999999999999115
100000000000000000049  99999999999999999249
100000000000000000047  99999999999999999391
100000000000000000045  99999999999999999541
100000000000000000043  99999999999999999699
100000000000000000041  99999999999999999865
100000000000000000039  0
100000000000000000037  184
100000000000000000035  376
100000000000000000033  576
100000000000000000031  784
```

So, we can see this number is p:

```
100000000000000000039  0
```

If we copy that number, we can set p equal to that and can set q equal to n over p:

```
>>> p = 100000000000000000039
>>> q = n/p
```

If we print, we will get the following:

```
>>> p
100000000000000000039L
>>> q
100000000000000000129L
>>> n
10000000000000000168000000000000000005031L
```

You can see n matches with p*q. So, we've now factored that long number into its complement primes.

Here's the first challenge:

> First challenge: Factor this number
>
> o 12345925929629679012962970370456791111122222098932964637053765599260929646321154446111289984805767

Here's the second challenge:

> Second challenge: Factor this number
>
> o 245731949077587003410793632769772440172121093648772379511569661065308222834597845272487909241946260280128792103441259245182932059730438317062685471060402660920755731093250407425954390905112220219921 9

In both cases, you will be able to factor them.

What's next?

Internet of Things (IoT) has a promising future and will soon connect billions of devices. For IoT, security has always been a major concern. But the good news is that cryptography offers various options to secure IOT from hackers; hence, it is a key to the coming era of IoT.

Cryptography within IoT

When we talk about using cryptography within IoT, we are talking about using cryptography across many layers of the communication stack. If we look at the OSI model, we can see that crypto is used at Layer 2 and up with linking operating at level 2, networking operating at layer 3, and transporting operating at layer 4:

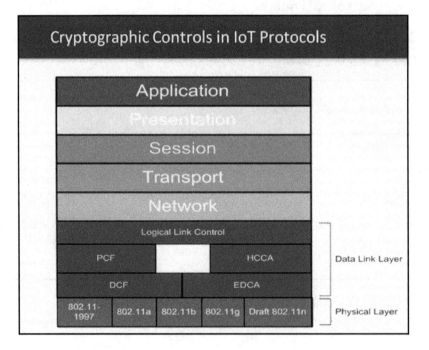

At the Application Layer, Cryptography is also used to protect communication through both authentication and encryption. Before we begin our description about specific cryptographic approaches for IOT protocols, let's first talk about the ready availability of exploitation tools for existing wireless protocols. As IOT matures, keep in mind that there are many tools available to exploit IOT wireless communication protocols and these tools will continue to rapidly keep up with new technologies introduced to support the IOT.

For example, looking at Wi-Fi 802.11, which was introduced in 1989, the AirCrack tool was introduced in 2004 and to this day is still a popular and well-supported tool. There are also many tools available to exploit Bluetooth communication and cellular communication.

Besides this, keys that drive crypto must be securely managed both at the device (module) level as well as throughout an enterprise. Let's explore some of them.

ZigBee cryptographic keys

ZigBee uses many keys for cryptographic operations:

- **Link key**: This is established based on the use of pre-provisioned master key from the manufacturer. The link key provides point-to-point secure connection between two ZigBee nodes. The link key is also used to establish derived keys, including data keys, key-transport keys, and Key-load keys
- **Key-transport keys**: This key is the outcome of executing the specialized keyed hash function under the link key with the 1-octet string 0x00 as the input string

Complexity of ZigBee key management

As mentioned earlier, key management is challenging. Let's take a look at how challenging key management can be. Take, for example, the ZigBee protocol. There are three primary types of keys that can be employed within the ZigBee network. Master keys are often preinstalled by the vendor and protect the exchange between two ZigBee nodes as they generate link keys. Link keys support node-to-node communication and network keys support broadcast communication.

Key management functions might be built into the media management software of utility, for example, and it might be provided as standalone software. However, all of these keys need to be sufficiently secured across their entire lifecycle.

Bluetooth – LE

The Bluetooth low energy protocol employs cryptography for pairing devices for future relationships. Bluetooth—LE uses various keys within these cryptographic processes, including a **long-term key** (**LTK**), which is used to generate a 128-bit key for the link layer encryption and a **connection signature resolving key** (**CSRK**), which is used for digitally signing data at the ATT layer.

With this, we come to the end of this book. Cryptography applications should be tailored specifically for the threat environments. Cryptography is based on strong, well- designed algorithms and associated with all layers of the communication stack. It is everywhere and fundamental to the security of IOT systems.

Summary

In this chapter, we covered AES, the strongest private key system in common use today, and its two modes, ECB and CBC. We covered the padding oracle attack against CBC, which is made possible when an error message gives the attacker more information than they should have about the encryption process.

Finally, we covered RSA, the primary public key algorithm in use today to send secrets over the internet, and we also looked at the challenge where we cracked RSA in the case where the two prime numbers are similar instead of being independent and randomly chosen. We also looked at the future of cryptography and how it will help secure IOT devices.

Other Books You May Enjoy

If you enjoyed this book, you may be interested in these other books by Packt:

Python Penetration Testing Cookbook

Rejah Rehim

ISBN: 978-1-78439-977-1

- Learn to configure Python in different environment setups
- Find an IP address from a web page using BeautifulSoup and Scrapy
- Discover different types of packet sniffing script to sniff network packets
- Master layer-2 and TCP/ IP attacks
- Master techniques for exploit development for Windows and Linux
- Incorporate various network- and packet-sniffing techniques using Raw sockets and Scrapy

Python for Offensive PenTest

Hussam Khrais

ISBN: 978-1-78883-897-9

- Code your own reverse shell (TCP and HTTP)
- Create your own anonymous shell by interacting with Twitter, Google Forms, and SourceForge
- Replicate Metasploit features and build an advanced shell
- Hack passwords using multiple techniques (API hooking, keyloggers, and clipboard hijacking)
- Exfiltrate data from your target
- Add encryption (AES, RSA, and XOR) to your shell to learn how cryptography is being abused by malware
- Discover privilege escalation on Windows with practical examples
- Countermeasures against most attacksld your own Windows IoT Face Recognition door locking system

Leave a review - let other readers know what you think

Please share your thoughts on this book with others by leaving a review on the site that you bought it from. If you purchased the book from Amazon, please leave us an honest review on this book's Amazon page. This is vital so that other potential readers can see and use your unbiased opinion to make purchasing decisions, we can understand what our customers think about our products, and our authors can see your feedback on the title that they have worked with Packt to create. It will only take a few minutes of your time, but is valuable to other potential customers, our authors, and Packt. Thank you!

Index

CPSIA information can be obtained
at www.ICGtesting.com
Printed in the USA
LVHW062006040621
689414LV00007B/111

9 781789 534443